GUARANTEED
GROWTH

MARCO GARCIA

GUARANTEED
GROWTH

8 PRINCIPLES FOR CHURCH AND ORGANIZATIONAL GROWTH

 THIS BOOK IS NOT FOR THE LEADER THAT IS CONTENT WITH THE RESULTS HE OR SHE ALREADY HAS.

XULON PRESS ELITE

Xulon Press Elite
2301 Lucien Way #415
Maitland, FL 32751
407.339.4217
www.xulonpress.com

© 2020 by Marco Garcia
Revised 2021

All rights reserved solely by the author. The author guarantees all contents are original and do not infringe upon the legal rights of any other person or work. No part of this book may be reproduced in any form without the permission of the author. The views expressed in this book are not necessarily those of the publisher.

Unless otherwise indicated, Scripture quotations are taken from The New Living Translation (NLT). Copyright © 1996, 2004, 2007 by Tyndale House Foundation. Used by permission. All rights reserved.

Paperback ISBN-13: 978-1-5456-6389-9
eBook ISBN-13: 978-1-5456-6390-5

DEDICATION

I dedicate this book to you, my loving mother. Mom, you are my best friend, mentor and inspiration. If it wasn't for you, I would not have written this book or be the person I am today. Thank you for all the sacrifices you made to pave the way for my success as a father, a husband and spiritual leader.
Thank you for not only introducing me to Jesus, but training me on how to serve and love Him with all my heart. Thank you for believing in me when it seemed no one else did. As a result, you developed in me the self-confidence I needed to step out and do what others believed was impossible.

Today I am a sold-out follower of Jesus Christ, loving father, faithful husband and Pastor of a thriving church, that is reaching thousands of people every day for Christ. You taught me how to be a servant leader. You also taught me the Word of God and that love is the most powerful force in the world to cause change in people's lives. I am so grateful for you and I love you so much!

PROVERBS 31:28 (ESV)

HER CHILDREN RISE UP AND CALL HER BLESSED; HER HUSBAND ALSO, AND HE PRAISES HER:

CONTENTS

WHAT DOES GUARANTEED GROWTH MEAN?   XIII

INTRODUCTION   XVII

PREVIEW   XXI

Chapter 1
Principle #1 – Love Creates The Atmosphere For Guaranteed Growth.   1

Chapter 2
How To Build Principle #1 – Three Steps To Create An Atmosphere Of Love For Guaranteed Growth   21

Chapter 3
Principle #2 – Doing What God Has Called Us To Do Leads To Guaranteed Growth   55

Chapter 4
How To Build Principle #2 – Six Facts About Growth Related To Our Calling   63

Chapter 5
Principle #3 – A Church That Finds And Meets Needs Is Guaranteed To Grow!   83

Chapter 6
How To Build Principle #3 – Two Insights
To Effectively Meeting Needs 93

CHAPTER 7
Principle #4 – A Church That Takes Care
Of The Poor Is Guaranteed To Grow! 105

Chapter 8
How To Build Principle #4 – Invite The Poor
And Unlock Two Growth Results 119

Chapter 9
Principle #5 – A Church That
Has An Excellent Children's Ministry
Is Guaranteed To Grow! 127

Chapter 10
How To Build Principle #5 – Ten Practical
Steps To Build A Successful Children's
Ministry 145

Chapter 11
Principle #6 – A Church That Finds A Place
For Everyone To Serve Is Guaranteed
To Grow! 155

Chapter 12
How To Build Principle #6 – Eight Practical
Steps To Building A Strong Servant Base 173

Chapter 13
Principle #7 – A Church That Preaches
The Gospel And Makes A Call To Respond
Is Guaranteed To Grow!   185

Chapter 14
How To Build Principle #7 – Five Steps To
Make A Successful Call To Salvation   191

Chapter 15
Principle #8 – A Church That Cares For
People Through Vibrant Small Groups
Is Guaranteed To Grow!   203

Chapter 16
How To Build Principle #8 – Eight Goals
Of A Small Group That Lead To
Guaranteed Growth   223

Chapter 17
Seven Steps To Start A Small Group
Ministry In Your Church   253

Bonus Section
HOW TO HELP PEOPLE OPEN UP IN SMALL GROUPS   259

Conclusion   267

x

This book is not for the leader that is content with the results he or she already has. This book will change the direction and the growth of your ministry forever!

Let's get ready to grow!

WHAT DOES GUARANTEED GROWTH MEAN?

Let's meditate on these definitions as we begin our growth journey...

GUARANTEED

A promise or assurance of a particular outcome, for sure, certain, in the bag, irrefutable, definite, unquestionable, absolute.

GROWTH

Increase in size and stage of development, something that has grown or developed by a process, expansion, enlargement, maturity, addition, multiplication, prosperity, success, build up.

DECLARATION: "I WANT GUARANTEED GROWTH"

GROWTH HAPPENS WHEN...

GROWTH HAPPENS WHEN SOULS ARE BEING SAVED AND ADDED TO THE KINGDOM OF GOD!

ACTS 2:41 (AMP)

"So then, those who accepted his message were baptized; and on that day about 3,000 souls were added [to the body of believers]."

GROWTH HAPPENS WHEN WE ARE MAKING DISCIPLES – FOLLOWERS OF JESUS CHRIST!

MATTHEW 28:19 (NLT)

"Therefore, go and make disciples of all the nations, baptizing them in the name of the Father and the Son and the Holy Spirit."

GROWTH HAPPENS WHEN WE ARE EQUIPPING GOD'S PEOPLE FOR THE WORK OF THE MINISTRY!

EPHESIANS 4:11-12 (NLT)

"Now these are the gifts Christ gave to the church: the apostles, the prophets, the evangelists, and the pastors and teachers. Their responsibility is to equip God's people to do his work and build up the church, the body of Christ."

GROWTH HAPPENS WHEN...

GROWTH HAPPENS WHEN OUR PEOPLE AND MINISTRIES ARE ACTIVELY INVITING PEOPLE TO COME TO CHURCH!

LUKE 14:23 (NLT)

"So his master said, 'Go out into the country lanes and behind the hedges and urge anyone you find to come, so that the house will be full.'"

GROWTH HAPPENS WHEN OUR CHURCHES AND PEOPLE ARE FULL OF GOD'S LOVE!

1 THESSALONIANS 3:12 (NLT)

"And may the Lord make your love for one another and for all people grow and overflow, just as our love for you overflows.

INTRODUCTION

Our Growth Story

After fifteen years of ministry, we are now doing fourteen services a week with a weekly attendance of over 7,000 people with over 100 active ministries. The purpose of this book is to share some of the principles we've learned in the last fifteen years that have attributed to our growth. The growth we have experienced has been achieved under adverse conditions or in other words, it has not been easy. We are in the City of San Bernardino, California, the second poorest large city in the country and California's most dangerous city. Most of the churches that start in this city close down within their first year of ministry because of the great poverty and limited resources available to help the people. In San Bernardino, the main economy is government assistance; 43.5% of the population in San Bernardino are on some type of welfare.[1] The city has gone through bankruptcy and has been in a state of trying to recover for 20 years. San Bernardino also had one of the highest murder rates per capita in the country and our local high school had over fifty percent

---

[1] (https://www.dailynews.com/2011/07/15/ranks-of-san-bernardino-county-welfare-recipients-grow-dramatically/)

of students dropping out. You might be asking, "Why go over all of these negative stats?" The answer to that question is simple; "If growth can happen here, it can happen anywhere!" Every community has its own difficulties and reasons why growth is not probable, but I thank God that He has given us His wisdom and favor to do the impossible with Him. We are honored to be a small part of the global church that is bringing hope to hurting and hopeless communities all over the world. It is also a great honor to be able to share with you some of the principles that God has given us that have produced Guaranteed Growth. Every day we are all learning. None of us know it all, but we can accelerate our personal growth as we share with one another what we have learned throughout our own personal journeys.

When we planted our church, we did it with little to no experience, but through a lot of hard work and trial and error. We have seen a steady pace of growth over the years. We started our church in an 8,000 sq. ft. facility and have now grown into doing ministry in a 120,000+ sq. ft. building which gives us the room to minister to thousands of people at one time. We have also opened our second campus, ten minutes away from our present location and within a two-month period of time; the second campus has grown to over 1,200 in weekly attendance. We have seen a pattern of consistent growth in every building that we have occupied and are believing that this will become the pattern for your church and ministry as well.

We are so excited to share the growth principles that have allowed us to achieve exponential growth over a relatively short period of time. All the principles that we will present to you in this book have been proven to cause Guaranteed Growth and will work for anyone and anywhere that they are applied.

PREVIEW

GROWTH IS FIRST A STATE OF MIND

God Commands us to Grow!

Maybe you are saying, "I am content with a small ministry and I don't want to grow."

Every growing leader needs to resist the temptation of agreeing with this anti-growth mindset and make sure that they are getting their mindset from the Word of God. We have all heard of the spirit of anti-Christ but there is also another spirit that is attacking the church and that is an anti-growth spirit. This spirit will do all it can to stop us and the church from growing. It is a surprise to many leaders that God doesn't recommend for us to grow, but He commands us to grow! Growth is a command.

GROWTH IS A COMMAND!

The only one that would not agree with this command to grow is the enemy. He does not want the kingdom of God to spread and the easiest way to do it is by influencing leaders to settle for the status quo. It is easy to be influenced by this anti-growth spirit because growth can be so challenging. The fact is that in order for our ministry organization to grow, we must grow out of every limiting mindset.

Before we dive into the principles that cause growth, we must build the faith that is needed to experience growth in our lives and ministries. Let's start out by looking deeper into the first command that God gave mankind.

> *Genesis 1:28 (NLT) – "Then God blessed them and said, 'Be **fruitful** and **multiply**. **Fill** the earth and govern it…'"*

This scripture is spoken in a way that leaves no doubt of what God's intentions were for mankind. God has blessed us to be fruitful and multiply.

> The word **fruitful** (Hebrew: parah) means to branch off, show fruit, grow and increase.
>
> The word **multiply** (Hebrew: rabah) means to become many, numerous, to make large, increase greatly, abundance.

The word **fill** (Hebrew: male) means to be full, replenish, be satisfied, to mass, overflow.

God uses these three words to confirm that growth was His original intent for every single human being and group of people. The good news is that whatever God commands us to do He gives us the ability to carry it out. Praise God!

God Expects Us To Grow!

God not only commands us to grow, He has also blessed and empowered us to grow! Growth is not just a great goal it is our God given destiny.

> **GROWTH IS NOT JUST A GREAT GOAL IT IS OUR GOD GIVEN DESTINY.**

God never creates anything without growth in mind, including a church or organization. If we are not growing, we are not walking in the full blessing that God has purposed for our lives and ministries. Our part in the growth process is to believe that growth is in our future and then use the talent, opportunities, and time that God has given us to create growth. For those who are still struggling with this concept of growth, you might be saying, "that was an Old Testament scripture."

In the New Testament, growth continues to be the theme. Jesus gives us a parable of the talents to drive the point home. To one he gave five talents, another two and another one talent, based on their ability. The expectations that Jesus had on these three servants, was the same. Invest what I have given you and create growth.

> *Matthew 25:14-30 (NKJV)... "15 And to one he gave five talents, to another two, and to another one, to each according to his own ability; and immediately he went on a journey..."*

One day, every one of us will give an account of what we have done with the gifts and talents he has entrusted us with. God doesn't expect us to grow at the same pace and levels, but he does expect us to grow.

> **GOD DOESN'T EXPECT US TO GROW AT THE SAME PACE AND LEVELS, BUT HE DOES EXPECT US TO GROW.**

Get ready to go to a place of exponential growth. There's no limit to what God will do for those that have determined to live a life of growth. God guarantees that if we're faithful with the little he's given us, he will give us more!

Matthew 25:23 (NKJV) – *"His lord said to him, 'Well done, good and faithful servant; you have been faithful over a few things, I will make you ruler over many things. Enter into the joy of your lord.'"*

Just like God expects us to grow, we should also have an expectation of growth in our ministries and organizations. In this parable we see that the two servants that expected to grow, invested what God gave them, doubled their talents, and were promoted to higher levels of leadership and influence to create greater growth for the kingdom of heaven. If it worked for them, it will work for us. Growth is for everyone!

There is a principle of growth that is highlighted in this scripture; **"Every servant that invests what he has will experience growth."** In this parable we do not see an example of a servant that invested what the master gave him without seeing a return on his investment. Both servants that invested doubled what they invested. After reading this book, every one of us will have 8 principles that we will be able to apply to our ministries that are guaranteed to create growth and increase.

> **"EVERY SERVANT THAT INVESTS WHAT HE HAS WILL EXPERIENCE GROWTH."**

There is another principle in this parable that we need to be aware of. This principle is given to us as a warning. The principle says that; **"Everyone that doesn't invest what God has given them will not see growth and even the little they have will be taken away from them."** Let's not be the one servant that did nothing with what God gave him. His story ends on a really sad note.

Matthew 25:24
"To those who use well what they are given, even more will be given, and they will have an abundance. But from those who do nothing, even what little they have will be taken away."

Ministries that refuse to grow and learn what it takes to increase, will end up in the same place as this wicked servant. Even the little they have will be taken away from them. It is a simple fact that if we are not growing we are dying. Any church that has chosen not to grow will begin to see a trend of decrease instead of increase. The few people they have, will begin to seek out opportunities for growth outside of their organization because every one of them instinctively know that growth is what they want. No one wants to be part of an organization that is not growing. Every one of us has a choice to make and that choice will determine whether we will have supernatural increase or supernatural decrease. Growth isn't luck, it is a choice. Today is the day that we need to agree with the Word of God and choose to be fruitful and multiply!

Ok, now that you have made a choice to grow and resisted the anti-growth spirit that tries to influence every believer and leader, it is time to learn. In this book we are going to learn 8 principles that are guaranteed to expand our faith and cause growth, if we apply them.

"The enemy doesn't attack us when we APPLAUD the Word, but when we APPLY it!"

"THE ENEMY DOESN'T ATTACK US WHEN WE APPLAUD THE WORD, BUT WHEN WE APPLY IT!"

CHAPTER ONE

PRINCIPLE #1 "LOVE CREATES AN ATMOSPHERE FOR GUARANTEED GROWTH"

CHAPTER 1

PRINCIPLE #1 – LOVE CREATES THE ATMOSPHERE FOR GUARANTEED GROWTH

1 Corinthians 14:1 (NLT)
"Let love be your highest goal!..."

We are living in a world with so much anger, division and heart break. Many of the people that we have contact with on a daily basis have not experienced a touch of love for years. If we would make love the "highest goal" in our churches and organizations, we would really stand out as a place that people would want to frequent and do business with.

Just like Disneyland is known as the "happiest place on earth," let's make it our goal to make our churches and organizations the "most loving places on earth." Any organization that has developed a culture of love has also become an attractive organization. We create a demand on our organization when we create an atmosphere of love because every person on earth has an innate desire to love and be loved. Love is the greatest need on earth and the good news is; our churches and organizations can meet that need.

In this chapter we are going to dive into this growth principle of love and learn how to develop an atmosphere of love which is guaranteed to cause growth. Love is the atmosphere of Guaranteed Growth, just like good soil is the prime condition for a seed to germinate. Our goal as a church is for everyone to absolutely feel loved after every interaction with us. The question we must constantly ask ourselves; "Did we love them to the best of our ability?" Love never fails! I have never heard of something that always succeeds and never fails, but God gives us a promise that love is guaranteed to work each and every time. Love comes with a fail proof guarantee! In other words, love always leads to success and growth. Let's start out with 6 Growth Guarantees tied to love.

LOVE COMES WITH A FAIL PROOF GUARANTEE!

1 Corinthians 13:8 (NIV)
Love never fails...

Fails: (Ekpipto) powerless, to fall to the ground without effect, to lose, become inefficient.

SIX LOVE GUARANTEES

Ephesians 3:19-20 (NLT)
"May you experience the love of Christ,
though it is too great to understand fully.
*Then you will be made **COMPLETE** with all the*
FULLNESS** of life and **POWER
that comes from God. 20 Now all glory to God,
who is able, through his
mighty power at work within us, to accomplish
*infinitely **MORE** than we might ask or think."*

There are four words that stand out in this particular portion of scripture. The words, COMPLETE, POWER, FULLNESS and MORE. All of these words have to do with growth and are dependent on experiencing the love of Christ. The love that causes Guaranteed Growth is qualified as the love of Christ. This is a love that we can only give if we have first received it by placing our faith in Christ as our Lord and Savior. This love is a love that is totally unselfish, unconditional and sacrificial. This is a love that can't be conquered and is always looking out for the well-being and advancement of those that are the objects of this love. We don't love in order to advance our churches or organization, we love to advance the people and then our organizations can't help but grow. Remember when the people grow, the organization grows. Creating an atmosphere where people can experience Christ's love is guaranteed to produce completeness, fullness, power and infinitely more! Let's look at these Love Guarantees a little closer.

> **WE DON'T LOVE IN ORDER TO ADVANCE OUR CHURCHES OR ORGANIZATION, WE LOVE TO ADVANCE THE PEOPLE AND THEN OUR ORGANIZATIONS CAN'T HELP BUT GROW.**

GUARANTEE #1 – COMPLETENESS

The word **"Complete"** is the Greek word (pleroo) and it means; to make full, to fill up, to cause to abound, to fill to the top or brim.

This scripture promises us that after we experience Christ's love, we will be made complete. There is also an assumption in this verse that every human is incomplete and the only thing that can fill that void is the love of God. If our churches and organizations are full of God's love, they will be seen as a place where people can receive wholeness, abundance and increase. Our churches and organizations will be like a gas station where they can come and be filled up with love. The pattern for completeness and growth is set, we create an atmosphere where people experience the unconditional love of Christ and after that comes fullness or another way to say it - growth! When love is in our atmosphere, completeness is also in our atmosphere and that means that everyone that comes into contact with this love is made complete. There is nothing like being exposed to the greatest power on earth, the power of Christ's love.

GUARANTEE #2 - POWER

The word **Power (dynamis)** is strength, ability, power for performing miracles, moral power, the power to influence and resources arising from numbers.

Love and power are always associated with each other. The Bible says that God "has not given us a spirit of fear, but LOVE, POWER and sound mind".

> *2 Timothy 1:7 (NKJV)*
> *For God has not given us a spirit of fear,*
> *but of POWER AND of LOVE*
> *and of a sound mind.*

This power is able to make people and our organization whole in the areas that have been incomplete or lacking. Even while I am writing about the love of Christ, I am experiencing the completeness and power of God that is supernaturally released anytime an atmosphere of love is created. I pray that you are experiencing it as well. The power that we can experience through the love of Christ is indescribable. Anytime Jesus was moved by His love and compassion for the people, the power of God flowed through Him and people were healed, set free and supernaturally provided for.

Matthew 14:14 (NLT)
Jesus saw the huge crowd as he stepped from the boat, and he had COMPASSION on them AND HEALED THEIR SICK.

The correlation is always the same love, compassion and then the power of God touches the needs of the people and causes miracles. Jesus never lacked a crowd because his ministry was always full of love and power. Could it be the next growth spurt in our organization is just waiting for the love atmosphere to be set so that the power of God can flow through us and touch the people with exactly what they need?

> **JESUS NEVER LACKED A CROWD BECAUSE HIS MINISTRY WAS ALWAYS FULL OF LOVE AND POWER.**

We as a church have seen the power of Christ's love work with every crowd in every building that we have been in. We have seen the power of God's love make people whole and as a result the church has been filled to the brim. We have outgrown our last 3 buildings and are now in our fourth building, because love always causes Guaranteed Growth and overflow.

GUARANTEE #3 – FULLNESS

The word **Fullness** is the Greek word (pleroma) and describes a ship that is full of sailors, rowers, soldiers and cargo; abundance, filled with the presence, power and riches of God.

The word is promising that we will be made complete "with all the fullness of life and power that comes from God." This fullness comes from experiencing the Love of Christ. As long as our churches and organizations are filled with the love of God, we will also be full of the presence, power and resources of God. We can't afford for our love to be snuffed out by being offended, angry or apathetic. If we let the love go, we also let the supernatural power, presence and provision of God go. When our churches and organizations are full of love, the people will begin to say; "There is something different about those people that I really like." The ship that is full of sailors, soldiers, cargo and riches represents our churches, ministries and businesses that are also full of love.

> AS LONG AS OUR CHURCHES AND ORGANIZATIONS ARE FILLED WITH THE LOVE OF GOD, WE WILL ALSO BE FULL OF THE PRESENCE, POWER AND RESOURCES OF GOD.

Any ship that becomes a "Love Boat", God promises to fill with His people, resources and power. God is looking for ships or vessels to carry His cargo to His intended destinations. Any person, organization or ministry that has intentionally made love their highest goal will experience the fullness that only comes from God. Remember God is in the referral business, He will only send His people and resources to organizations that will take care of them with His love. Let's create an atmosphere that God can fill with His presence, power and provision. There will always be fullness of life and growth in any place where there is an atmosphere full of God's love. Love and fullness go hand in hand. You can't have one without the other.

GUARANTEE #4 – MORE (Infinitely more than we can ask or think.)

The Greek word for **"Infinitely More"** is (hyper) which means: beyond, more than, over and above, exceedingly, immeasurably great, unlimited, unbounded, abundantly, heavenly.

God promises to accomplish "infinitely more" than we can ask or think through the "mighty power" working within us. The "mighty power" described in this scripture that works within us, is the love of Christ. When we allow His love to flow through us and our organizations,

He guarantees to blow our minds with "infinitely more than we can ask or think". The limits that have hindered our growth in the past will be removed so that God can do everything He desires to accomplish in us and our organizations. God will remove the limits that have stifled our creativity, the limits on our finances and limits that have been barriers to increase. What God wants to do in our lives and organizations is greater than our limited vision. His thoughts are always higher than ours. We don't need to fear that if we do it God's way we will experience less; more is God's original idea, not ours. Any organization that creates a culture of love will experience infinitely more! Remember the atmosphere of love is the atmosphere of heaven, and there are no limits in heaven. So let's take the limits off our church, ministries and organizations by making a decision to grow in our love for God and the people. Love always creates more!

> **ANY ORGANIZATION THAT CREATES A CULTURE OF LOVE WILL EXPERIENCE INFINITELY MORE!**

GUARANTEE #5 - GAIN

We can't get away from the connection between love and growth. In the scripture below we see it again. Love is associated with the word "gain." The main point of this scripture is that without love there will not be any true "gain."

> *1 Corinthians 13:3 (NLT)*
> *If I gave everything I have to the poor and even sacrificed my body,*
> *I could boast about it; but if I didn't love others, I would have **GAINED** nothing.*

Definition of **Gain**: increase, profit, progress, advantage, success, power and influence.

Any activity or business endeavor where Christ's love is not the motive will have no real gain. We can do really great works and implement great ideas, but if we do them without love for the people we are serving or working with, there will not be any meaningful gain.

We have all heard the saying, "No pain No gain." But I am going to introduce you to a new saying, "No love, No gain!" This statement might explain why we can be working really hard and implementing new ideas and still not experiencing any increase. God loves us too much to allow us to succeed without His love working through us and our organizations. True success, progress and profit always follow God's love. Let's not be one of those churches or organizations that has lost its first love and is now doing good deeds without the love of Christ. It is so easy to start out full of love and end up apathetic.

> **TRUE SUCCESS, PROGRESS AND PROFIT ALWAYS FOLLOW GOD'S LOVE.**

Revelation 2:4 (NLT)
"But I have this complaint against you.
You don't love me or each other as you did at first!

All of us are searching for new methods and the right people to help our organizations grow, but without love it won't work! A ministry or organization that has lost its love motive will soon experience loss. Loss of great employees, loss of faithful members and a decrease in resources. Thank God that we can turn it around by just renewing our commitment to make love our highest goal again. Making love our greatest goal puts us into position for our greatest gains, greatest harvest of souls, greatest move of God, greatest profits, greatest attendance and greatest influence in our community. The future is bright for any church or organization that makes love for God and his people its highest goal!

> **MAKING LOVE OUR GREATEST GOAL PUTS US INTO POSITION FOR OUR GREATEST GAINS.**

GUARANTEE #6 - ENCOUNTERS WITH GOD

Encounters with God is the most important guarantee of all. This guarantee is crucial for all churches, ministries and organizations that have made establishing God's purpose on earth their mission. The main mission of heaven is to see the lost saved for eternity through the preaching of the Good News of Jesus Christ. We want everyone that comes into our churches, ministries and organizations to have supernatural encounters with God. There is nothing more important in the whole world than our people having encounters with God's love that will eventually lead them to develop a relationship with Him. If we are just interested in the growth of our churches and ministries without our people having encounters with God, we have truly been deceived. All the gains in the world mean nothing if in the process they have lost their souls for eternity.

Mark 8:36 (NLT)
And what do you benefit if you gain the whole world but lose your own soul?

We want our growth and gains to surpass this life and go on into eternity. How sad would it be that our churches are full of people who don't know Jesus as their Lord and Savior. We can all fall into a trap that makes us think that all that matters is our present life and our temporary gains. God's main purpose for sharing His love is to save mankind and give them the free gift of eternal life. He desires that every one of us live for Him now and be with Him for eternity.

John 3:16 (NKJV)
For God so loved the world that He gave His only begotten Son,
that whoever believes in Him should not perish but have everlasting life.

Unless a person believes in Jesus as their Savior and receives the free gift of eternal life, they have not gained anything that will last beyond this life. We don't just want members in our churches and employees in our businesses, we want people that have had God encounters that lead to supernatural conversions.

> **WE DON'T JUST WANT MEMBERS IN OUR CHURCHES AND EMPLOYEES IN OUR BUSINESSES, WE WANT PEOPLE THAT HAVE HAD GOD ENCOUNTERS THAT LEAD TO SUPERNATURAL CONVERSIONS.**

We have been conditioned to think that we need to separate God and business. I am afraid that even churches have been affected by this mindset and are no longer loving people enough to let them know the true condition of their souls without Christ. The truth is all of us have sinned, or another way to say it, we have all broken God's laws. Just like breaking one of the laws of our earthly government will lead to fines and penalties, there are also consequences for breaking God's laws.

The penalty for breaking just one of God's laws is death, which really means eternal separation from God in a miserable place called hell. The good news is that God loved us so much that he sent His only son to pay the price for our spiritual crimes. Yes! Jesus died for us. He took on the punishment that we deserved. The penalties and punishment due to us was fully paid for by the sufferings and death of Jesus Christ on the cross. The Good News is that every one of us can be forgiven and receive the free gift of eternal life by faith in Jesus Christ.

Receiving the free gift of eternal life is easy. All we have to do is admit that we are sinners deserving punishment, exhibit a willingness to turn from our sinful lives, and place our faith in Jesus Christ for the forgiveness of our sins and salvation. It is as easy as one, two and three.

If you would like to be forgiven of all your sins and receive the free gift of eternal life, repeat this prayer after me:

"Lord, I thank you for loving me so much that you sent your one and only Son Jesus to live, suffer and die for the punishment for my sins. I admit that I am a sinner that deserves to pay for the sins that I have committed, but I place my faith in Christ and the sacrifice He made for my sins. Today, I receive the free gift of forgiveness and eternal life by believing that Jesus paid the full price for my sins and that He conquered death when He resurrected. Today, I confess that Jesus is my personal Lord and Savior. Thank you Jesus for saving me!"

Without the love of God, the atmosphere is not set for prayers like this to be made and the greatest miracle of all to happen, the salvation of a soul for eternity. An atmosphere without love is an atmosphere without God, because God is love. Without love we can only offer a dead, religious experience with no power to transform lives for eternity.

We are living in a society full of agnostics and atheists. One encounter with God can turn that around. They are just looking for proof. Love is the undeniable proof of God's existence. Again, God is love!!

LOVE IS THE UNDENIABLE PROOF OF GOD'S EXISTENCE.

1 John 4:8 (ESV)
Anyone who does not love does not know God,
because GOD IS LOVE.

When people experience the passionate love of God through believers, they are literally having an encounter with God himself. They cannot deny their own experience. They will say, "It is true. When I came into that atmosphere, I felt a love that I have never felt before. What is that?" We will be able to answer: "The love you have experienced is God. You have just had an encounter with God." No one is going to be won over to faith in God through an argument, they must have their own real encounter with God for themselves. The Word of God and His love is what convinces a non-believer that God exists. Let's not deny them that experience by allowing the enemy to destroy our love through division, strife, anger, unforgiveness or apathy.

Our churches and organizations need to be known as the most loving places in our community. The Good News is that we can create an atmosphere of supernatural growth by just making love our highest goal. Love is the soil that all spiritual seeds grow in. Without creating an atmosphere of love, all the principles that we will learn in this book will not work.

LOVE IS THE SOIL THAT ALL SPIRITUAL SEEDS GROW IN.

Now that we have established that love is the atmosphere of growth, let's learn how to create this atmosphere of love in our churches and organizations.

CHAPTER TWO

HOW TO BUILD PRINCIPLE #1
THREE STEPS TO CREATE AN ATMOSPHERE OF LOVE

CHAPTER 2

HOW TO BUILD PRINCIPLE #1

THREE STEPS TO CREATE AN ATMOSPHERE OF LOVE FOR GUARANTEED GROWTH

STEP #1 - START TEACHING AND SPEAKING ON THE SUBJECT OF LOVE.

Once we have decided to make love our highest goal, our next step is to make the subject of love part of our everyday conversations and culture. What we are talking about is who we are and who we are becoming. This is a good time to look at our mission statements and vision statements and make sure that the word "love" is included. This is a subject that we cannot over-teach. When Jesus was asked; "Which was the most important commandment?", Jesus answered with intense clarity.

Matthew 22:37-39 (NLT)
Jesus replied, "'You MUST LOVE the Lord your GOD with all your heart, all your soul, and all your mind.'

38 This is the first and greatest commandment. 39 A second is equally important:
'LOVE YOUR NEIGHBOR as yourself.'

Jesus said that there is nothing more important than loving God and loving people. Love will never be the driving force in our churches and organizations until we bring it to the forefront. A great way to bring it to the forefront is to start a teaching series on Love. God's love will never be activated in the people, without intentional teaching on this subject. Jesus has commissioned every believer to love and teach His love commandments.

This is a subject that we cannot over-preach. When Jesus was asked, what was the greatest commandment, he gave us clear instruction, that we should love God and love our neighbor as ourselves. When we are teaching our congregation and ministries about love, we are discipling the people to be like Jesus. And when the church becomes like Jesus, we start getting the results of Jesus. We must be committed to continue to preach and teach the gospel of love, until there is a love-shift in our church. The series doesn't end until the atmosphere has changed. The standard of love that the church will walk in will be determined by the level of teaching that they receive.

> **WE MUST BE COMMITTED TO CONTINUE TO PREACH AND TEACH THE GOSPEL OF LOVE, UNTIL THERE IS A LOVE-SHIFT IN OUR CHURCH.**

TEACH IT!

Matthew 28:20 (NLT)
"Teach these new disciples to obey all the commands I have given you. And be sure of this: I am with you always, even to the end of the age."

LIVE IT!

John 13:34 (NLT)
So now I am giving you a new commandment: Love each other.
Just as I have loved you, you should love each other.

God promises He will be with us "even to the end of the age," if we will walk in His love and teach others His love commands. That means that any generation in any geographical location that teaches and exemplifies the love of God will also experience the promise of God's manifested presence and power. He will show up to transform hearts and lives.

You might be asking, "When do we stop teaching on the subject of God's love?" The answer is, "Never!" We must make a commitment to continue to teach and display the "Love of Jesus" until Jesus Christ comes back to take us all home. Teaching the Word with God's love will cause an obvious "love shift" in our church and organization. Once the atmosphere has been changed through the teaching, we must continue to pepper every sermon and lesson with the love of God. Our goal should be to do everything with the Love of God. This love shift will eventually show up in the way our staff and people are beginning to treat each other.

We will know that the atmosphere has shifted when we begin to hear testimonies from the people that they have never felt so loved. Our guests will say that as soon as they stepped on to the premises and had their first encounter with one of our volunteers or staff, they experienced God's love without judgment. Let's give the people what they need the most and that's the love of God that will cause them to supernaturally grow. This will also lead to Guaranteed Growth in our organization. The saddest thing in the world is a church without love because a church without love is a church without God. After teaching on love, the next step is to love and train our leaders and staff to lead this love revolution by their personal example.

> **THE SADDEST THING IN THE WORLD IS A CHURCH WITHOUT LOVE BECAUSE A CHURCH WITHOUT LOVE IS A CHURCH WITHOUT GOD.**

STEP #2 – LEADERS MUST EXEMPLIFY GOD'S LOVE IN ACTION.

The leaders in our church must be the ***love example***. Teaching is still not enough, it must be backed up with a healthy dose of modeling the desired behavior. Jesus trained his disciples to love, by living a life filled with Love.

Ephesians 5:1-2 (NLT)
"Imitate God, therefore, in everything you do, because you are his dear children. 2 Live a life filled with love, following the example of Christ. He loved us and offered himself as a sacrifice for us, a pleasing aroma to God."

Love must be displayed in a way that can be seen through action. When people see the smiles, hugs, patience, and the unconditional love we walk in, they will be impacted in such a way that it will cause them to begin to respect us and will build a desire within them to imitate the qualities that have been modeled before them.

Jesus showed us how to teach through example. Jesus never taught divine truth without walking it out in the flesh. The Word must always become flesh. May we be the flesh example of love for those that we are leading.

John 1:14 (NIV)
The Word became flesh and made his dwelling among us. We have seen his glory, the glory of the one and only Son, who came from the Father, full of grace and truth.

We must ask ourselves, have we given an example of love for our congregations or organizations to follow? In the last days of Jesus' life on earth, He drove this point home by washing his disciples' feet. Washing feet is one of the most selfless, loving and humble things anyone can ever do. After Jesus washed their feet, He said; "I have given you an example to follow."

John 13:15 (NLT)
"I have given you an example to follow, do as I have done unto you."

THE CONGREGATION AND THOSE IN OUR ORGANIZATION WILL ALWAYS MIRROR THE QUALITIES THEY SEE DISPLAYED IN THEIR LEADERS.

The congregation and those in our organization will always mirror the qualities they see displayed in their leaders. The people will never develop a healthy love walk unless they have seen it in their leadership. Our lives, as leaders should challenge the people to walk at a higher level of love. As we are imitating God, the people will eventually imitate us.

1 Corinthians 11:1 (NLT)
"And you should imitate me, just as I imitate Christ."

Anytime we enter into a church or organization that is filled with love, joy and excitement, it is a direct by-product of the leadership. Leadership should never blame the people that they are leading for not demonstrating qualities they have never lived out in front of them. The people will only reflect the lifestyles that have been modeled before them.

The spirit of the leader will be duplicated in the people. If we do not like what we see in the people, we might need to look at ourselves in the mirror. Our organizations will always be a representation of what we have taught and lived out in front of them.

Teaching love will always be a lot easier than living love, because living love will demand that we practice self-denial. In order to walk in love, we must deny ourselves from walking in a spirit of pride, anger, impatience, religion and judgment and choose to put on humility, kindness, patience and continual forgiveness.

Love will always be a choice, just like the clothes we chose to wear today. Love is more than an emotion, it's a decision! We make a decision to walk in love, even when we don't feel it. We are finally maturing, when we are being led by the spirit of God and not our feelings or circumstances.

LOVE IS MORE THAN AN EMOTION, IT'S A DECISION!

Leader, the scripture below is the standard for the lifestyle of love we should display with one another. Please do not just skim over this scripture. Look at every single word written and meditate and practice it, until it becomes our new standard.

Colossians 3:12-14 (MSG)
"So, chosen by God for this new life of love, dress in the wardrobe God picked out for you: compassion, kindness, humility, quiet strength, discipline. Be even-tempered, content with second place, quick to forgive an offense. Forgive as quickly and completely as the Master forgave you. And regardless of what else you put on, wear love. It's your basic, all-purpose garment. Never be without it."

Any shift in culture must begin in the highest levels of our organization which always seems to be the most challenging place to keep the unity. The way we treat our employees and each other as leaders and staff, will be how they will treat one another. It's so easy to let our guard down with those that we are closest to and see on a regular basis. Creating a love atmosphere means that anytime we have differences among ourselves, we need to immediately do all we can to settle them in order to keep the unity and love flowing.

Ephesians 4:2-3 (NLT)
"Always be humble and gentle. Be patient with each other, making allowance for each other's faults because of your love. ³ Make every effort to keep yourselves united in the Spirit, binding yourselves together with peace."

Even if it means that a ministry assignment is temporarily delayed. Loving and unified relationships must be our highest priority. Without loving relationships, we can't have healthy churches and organizations that are growing. Before we see the numbers increase, the love must increase within our leadership ranks and that will only happen as we wrestle with our own shortcomings and make every effort to keep ourselves united.

> **BEFORE WE SEE THE NUMBERS INCREASE, THE LOVE MUST INCREASE WITHIN OUR LEADERSHIP RANKS.**

STEP #3 - INTENTIONALLY PUT PEOPLE IN PLACE WITH LOVE ASSIGNMENTS.

Let's make love an appointment, not an accident.

THREE LOVE ASSIGNMENTS TO BUILD AN ATMOSPHERE OF LOVE IN OUR CHURCH

LOVE ASSIGNMENT #1 - PLACE GREETERS IN STRATEGIC SPOTS.

> *2 Corinthians 13:12 (NLT)*
> *"Greet each other with Christian love."*

Greek definition of Greet: (Aspazomai) – To draw to oneself, wish well to, welcome, to receive joyfully and embrace.

If the angels in heaven have a massive celebration every time one soul comes into the kingdom, we should also celebrate each and every person that God has given us the privilege to interact with. We are heaven's welcoming committee. When we welcome people with love and enthusiasm our guests get the message that God really loves them.

The people that we are greeting, will make an assumption about God based on how we treat them. Why would they want to receive our God, when they are unimpressed with our love for them? We are in the business of loving people into the kingdom of heaven. Let's break every stereotype that has been placed over Christians; let's show people that we are not judgmental, hypocritical, and religious. Love breaks down all the barriers that the enemy has put up between us and a hurting world. Everyone wants to be loved and celebrated! I've seen breakthroughs happen in just a hand-shake or a hug. Jesus told us that when people see our good works they will glorify God. Our acts of kindness are somehow always associated with what people think about God.

Matthew 5:16 (ESV)
In the same way, let your light shine before others, so that they may see your good works and give glory to your Father who is in heaven.

For us to be effective in this love assignment we must be intentional. Here are some practical guidelines that we use in our greeting ministry.

> **FOR US TO BE EFFECTIVE IN THIS LOVE ASSIGNMENT WE MUST BE INTENTIONAL.**

A rule of thumb is that our guest should be greeted at least five times during their worship experience. They should be greeted approximately three times before they are seated and two times while they are exiting the premises. Each one of these greetings will drive a point home, that we love them and so does God.

The first experience that our guest will have with a greeter will be with our parking lot team. Everyone on our parking lot team is hand-picked and they all have a few things in common, they have the gift of hospitality, a great love for people and beautiful smiles. Not everyone can represent the church at this critical place in ministry. The parking lot team is not only responsible for helping park cars and direct traffic, they are also there to establish a loving first impression. God has called a group of people to each one of our churches and organizations that are super gifted in helping people feel loved and feel welcomed.

Building an effective hospitality team will not be done accidentally. We should constantly be recruiting and training the best people to represent our church and organization in this important role of initial interaction.

Before our guests hear a word spoken by the pastor or a song sung by the worship team, they are already deciding whether this is a place where they belong. I have personally had people tell me that they decided to make our church their home before the worship service started based on the love they experienced from our greeting and hospitality team. Since we only have one opportunity to make a first impression, we should spend a great amount of time strategizing the best places to put our greeters. Around every corner, there should be someone with a love assignment, with the goal of making someone feel loved and welcomed.

Another way we make sure that everyone is greeted, is to set a time aside during our worship services for the whole congregation to greet each other.

Setting aside this time has a two-fold blessing. The first part of the blessing is that it creates an opportunity for everyone to get involved in receiving and giving love. The congregation is now going out of their way to welcome and embrace their brothers and sisters in their house of worship or ministry. Our church members should never get to the point that they are so self-consumed that they are unaware of the people that God has placed around them.

The second part of this two-fold blessing is that during this time of greeting the church culture is built and reinforced. After the greeting time is over, friends have been made, names have been exchanged, and everyone practiced being hospitable. Only what we practice over and over will become culture or second nature. We need to intentionally create time slots in our order of service for the values we want to be part of our culture. This culture of welcoming each other can also be established in our homes and places of business. In my own home, we have made it a rule that whoever enters a room should acknowledge and greet all who are there.

As a pastor, one of the practical ways that I show love is by walking down the aisle, smiling, waving, hugging, and expressing my love to as many people as I can during our time of greeting. I am not waiting for the people to come to me, I go to them. I am doing my best to send them a message that they are absolutely loved and valued. My greeting inspiration is Jesus. He took greeting to a whole new level by humbling himself as a leader and washing His disciples' feet.

> **I AM NOT WAITING FOR THE PEOPLE TO COME TO ME, I GO TO THEM. I AM DOING MY BEST TO SEND THEM A MESSAGE THAT THEY ARE ABSOLUTELY LOVED AND VALUED.**

Today, we can practice washing people's feet by the love we show them as they come from their dusty roads of pain, suffering and stress in their daily lives. It's an honor to be chosen by God to love, serve and enthusiastically welcome His people.

Our guest should be wowed by the display of love that they are receiving from the congregants and the leaders of our church or organization. We want to create a buzz where the people are saying; "My church and leaders are so loving. They always make me feel at home and that's why I come here."

Let's not underestimate or trivialize the time we've set aside to greet one another. This is a time where God is loving and taking care of His people through us.

John 21:16 (NLT)
"...If you love me take care of my sheep."

This is also a time where the whole congregation gets involved in the love appointment; where they are now going out of their way to welcome and embrace their brothers and sisters in their house of worship or ministry.

LOVE ASSIGNMENT #2 - CREATE A TIME AND PLACE FOR PEOPLE TO BE PRAYED FOR

There are many creative ways to include prayer in our church culture. Having a time and place for prayer should be one of our top priorities. Jesus said;

Matthew 21:13 (ESV)
. . . 'My house shall be called a house of prayer.

That means that the church should be a place where people can come to connect with God. Creating a culture of prayer is the same as creating a culture of love. As we open up the door for prayer, we will discover that our people are hurting and are desperate for a touch of God. Maybe during that week, they lost a loved one, had a miscarriage, got laid off from their job or were recently diagnosed with cancer. Making room for personal prayer is like throwing out a life preserver to those that are drowning in an ocean of heart break, hopelessness and pain. It would be unloving and definitely criminal to not give them an opportunity to connect with God through a loving prayer. I believe that one of the most neglected areas of ministry in our churches is prayer. We are really good at preparing great messages and worship experiences, but have neglected one of the most loving and powerful things we can do and that's extending our hearts to a broken world and connecting them to loving God through prayer.

> **MAKING ROOM FOR PERSONAL PRAYER IS LIKE THROWING OUT A LIFE PRESERVER TO THOSE THAT ARE DROWNING IN AN OCEAN OF HEART BREAK, HOPELESSNESS AND PAIN.**

One of the most loving things we can ever do is praying for someone who is in great need or going through a really difficult time in their lives. If we are going to be effective in this area of prayer, we must intentionally make time for it.

In our church we have created a moment of prayer in every one of our worship services. This is a time where we give our people an opportunity to come forward to receive prayer from one of our trained prayer counselors. These prayer counselors serve as an extended hand of God that is reaching out to them to comfort them in their moments of suffering and heart break. Their loving touch allows our people to experience the love of God in a very real way. The prayer counselors have three major responsibilities with the people that they are serving.

The first responsibility is obvious; make the person they are praying for feel loved.

The second major responsibility is to find out the needs of the people and pray with them. God has chosen to do everything through prayer and nothing apart from it. Prayer opens the door for the people to receive a miracle from God. While we are praying for the people they are going to receive miracles of healing, salvation, freedom from lifelong addictions and supernatural comfort and direction from the Holy Spirit.

The third major responsibility is to introduce them to their next step of spiritual growth. Our prayer counselors need to be trained and informed on the growth track that the church has created to disciple the people into spiritual maturity.

If we do not have a clear growth journey, it's really important for us to spend some time creating one. Without a growth track our prayer counselors, leaders and present congregation will not be able to direct the new convert or church member to their next step of spiritual growth. The growth track is intended to develop our church members into spiritually mature believers that know God, know His Word and know their purpose in the church body.

Having the right people in place with this love assignment will make all the difference in the world. Our goal is that the people have an encounter with God and prayer is one of the best ways for that to happen. When we make the call for the people to come forward to be saved, healed and seek God for wisdom and support, we are opening up the windows of heaven over their lives. Jesus is walking through every one of our churches and organizations desiring to share His love and blessings with people. This time of prayer allows Him an opportunity do so.

> **HAVING THE RIGHT PEOPLE IN PLACE WITH THIS LOVE ASSIGNMENT WILL MAKE ALL THE DIFFERENCE IN THE WORLD.**

This love assignment can also be accomplished in the market place. Our ministry life doesn't only exist when we are at church, it actually continues when we walk off our church campus. We are living in a world where people are overwhelmed, depressed and suffering from all kinds of emotional and relational pain. We can create a culture of prayer and care everywhere we set our feet. The majority of Jesus' ministry life was done on the streets not in the four walls of his local synagogue. One of the biggest impacts we can make on someone's life is discovering their greatest need and letting them know that we are going to pray for them and lovingly support them through their crisis.

In all the years that I was in the business world, I never had anyone reject prayer when they were facing a major challenge in their life. On the contrary, I was surprised by how grateful they were. Just think about it. Out of all the people that they know on earth, I was probably the only person concerned enough to pray for them. What a great display of God's love.

No matter what the case might be, we know that creating opportunities for people to open up and receive prayer is one of the greatest way we can show people that we love them.

LOVE ASSIGNMENT #3 - INVITE THEM TO JOIN OUR INNER CIRCLE

Every person on earth is yearning to be part of an inner circle of friends. Everyone is trying to find a place where they belong. We can meet that deep desire to belong by intentionally inviting people to join our inner circles and train them to do the same for others.

Inviting others into our inner circles is a love assignment that the whole congregation can participate in. Anytime we are inviting people to come into our inner circles, we are loving them in one of the most practical ways possible. Inviting others into our inner circles is as easy as inviting someone to have some coffee with us, inviting them to join our small group home bible study or asking them to participate in a ministry that we are involved in. Inviting others into our inner circle must become part of our church and organizational culture if we are going to experience Guaranteed Growth.

> **INVITING OTHERS INTO OUR INNER CIRCLE MUST BECOME PART OF OUR CHURCH AND ORGANIZATIONAL CULTURE IF WE ARE GOING TO EXPERIENCE GUARANTEED GROWTH.**

A sure way to build this culture is by integrating the inner circle invitation as part of our standard worship experience. Every time we highlight a ministry, a small group and give them a real opportunity to join, we are building the church and establishing the culture.

Culture is built by keeping our values at the forefront of everything we do. We must consistently present real opportunities for our people to connect and come into our inner circles.

With every invitation that is made we must also have practical steps they can take to join. Some examples are; a connection card they can fill out, an easy step by step process on our website, app, or a connection counter in our foyer filled with connection specialists. A connection specialist is someone we have trained for the specific purpose of bringing people into our inner circles.

Everywhere that our guests or members turn they should run into invitations to join our inner circles; our church members are inviting them, our announcements are inviting them, our website is inviting them, our ministries are inviting them, our leaders are inviting them, and in our foyer and parking lots they are also being invited.

Jesus built His inner circle of 12 by inviting them to be part of His life.

> **JESUS BUILT HIS INNER CIRCLE OF 12 BY INVITING THEM TO BE PART OF HIS LIFE.**

Matthew 4:18-22 (NIV)
As Jesus was walking beside the Sea of Galilee, he saw two brothers, Simon called Peter and his brother Andrew. They were casting a net into the lake, for they were fishermen. 19 "Come, follow me," Jesus said, "and I will send you out to fish for people." 20 At once they left their nets and followed him. 21 Going on from there, he saw two other brothers, James son of Zebedee and his brother John. They were in a boat with their father Zebedee, preparing their nets. Jesus called them, 22 and immediately they left the boat and their father and followed him.

Jesus not only invited people to join His inner circle, He commands us to go out and invite them as well.

> *Luke 14:23 (CJB)*
> *The master said to the slave, 'Go out to the country roads and boundary walls, and insistently persuade people to come in, so that my house will be full.*

The fact is people won't be part of our inner circles unless they are invited. Inviting others from the outer circles to our inner circles is how a church or organization grows healthy and strong. Any church or organization that is intentional about inviting others to join their inner circles is Guaranteed to Grow!!

Now that we have discussed how developing a love atmosphere comes with promised growth and have also explored some practical ways to build a love culture, we can now look at some major benefits that accompany a love atmosphere. Every one of these benefits describe attributes that every church and kingdom organization has to have in order to experience Guaranteed Growth.

THREE MAJOR BENEFITS OF CREATING A LOVE ATMOSPHERE

BENEFIT #1 – JOY!

> *John 15:11-12 (NLT)*
> *"I have told you these things so that you will be filled with my joy.*

Yes, your joy will overflow!
12 This is my commandment:
Love each other in the same way I have loved you."

Any church or organization that is full of God's love will also experience an overflow of God's joy! This is an amazing revelation. Love and joy always come together! We can't have one without the other. We see this association with love and joy even when the apostle Paul gives us a list of the fruits of the Spirit. He mentions love first and following love comes joy.

Galatians 5:22 (NLT)
"But the Holy Spirit produces this kind of fruit
in our lives: LOVE, JOY,
peace, patience, kindness, goodness, faithfulness,"

We are living in a world that is so depressed, angry, and fearful. When people come into our churches and kingdom businesses, they are hoping to find an answer to their emotional emptiness. They don't need another pill for their depression. All they need is a healthy dose of a church that is full of God's love and the overflowing joy of the Lord. I don't think there is anything more attractive and electric than people full of the joy of the Lord. A believer that is overflowing with joy is the best advertisement there is to promote Christ and our church. Who wouldn't want to be in an atmosphere where there is great love and great joy? Everyone is looking for that! God promises every one of us, that if we walk in love for others, we will also experience an overflow of his joy in our lives. This point cannot be over emphasized.

> **A BELIEVER THAT IS OVERFLOWING WITH JOY IS THE BEST ADVERTISEMENT THERE IS TO PROMOTE CHRIST AND OUR CHURCH.**

A church without love, will be a church without joy. Could it be we have been working on the symptoms and not the root of the problem? We have been so busy trying to teach our people how to overcome depression, fear, and anger and all we needed to do was teach them how to love. Whenever a believer neglects Jesus' command to love others the way He loved us, by default he has chosen to walk in depression, anger, and fear. The solution is clear, love must be our highest goal and as a result, love will heal the rest of our emotional dysfunctions. Love always has the power to heal, make us whole emotionally and fill our hearts with joy. In conclusion, a church full of love will be a church full of joy and a church full of joy will become a church full of people.

BENEFIT #2 - CREATE AN UNSELFISH CULTURE OF SACRIFICIAL LOVE

John 15:12-13 (NLT)
"This is my commandment: Love each other in the same way I have loved you. 13 There is no greater love than to lay down one's life for one's friends."

A church that is full of God's love will also practice sacrificial acts of love. Imagine an atmosphere where the people have one goal—to make sure everyone experiences the love of God even it means that they may have to sacrifice a personal preference. Any church or organization that practices sacrificial love will always see increase and growth! There is no limit to what God can do in an atmosphere like that. Love recreates the atmosphere of the original church, from the book of Acts. The first church practiced sacrificial love to the fullest. They were willing to give up everything they had so that all the needs of fellow believers would be met. With sacrificial love comes automatic growth.

WITH SACRIFICIAL LOVE COMES AUTOMATIC GROWTH.

Acts 2:47 (NLT)
"All the while praising God and enjoying the goodwill of all the people. And each day the Lord added to their fellowship those who were being saved."

Goodwill: Sacrificial acts of love and kindness; benevolence (desire to do good to others; charitableness).

The atmosphere was set for growth. Just like love and joy always come together so does goodwill and growth. The scripture above says that while they were enjoying the goodwill of all the people, the Lord ADDED TO THEIR FELLOWSHIP. Addition follows sacrificial acts of love. A church that practices sacrificial love will always see supernatural growth.

> **A CHURCH THAT PRACTICES SACRIFICIAL LOVE WILL ALWAYS SEE SUPERNATURAL GROWTH.**

BENEFIT #3 – AN ACTIVATION OF THE SUPERNATURAL POWER OF GOD

When we put people in an atmosphere full of God's love, they will begin to get healed, delivered, set free, and saved. An atmosphere of love sets the stage for God to perform. Jesus is our example of how love always precedes a manifestation of the supernatural.

Everything Jesus did was motivated by love. Even the feeding of the multitude was motivated by compassion and love. Before Jesus does the miracle of multiplying the seven loaves of bread and few fish to feed thousands of people, He makes a qualifying statement; " I have compassion on the multitude". Jesus is pointing us to a major key to unlock the supernatural power of God and that's Love. The pattern is always the same; love first then miracles. When our motive is compassion and love for the people, we will always see God put his blessing on it, which will result in a supernatural display of God's power.

> **WHEN OUR MOTIVE IS COMPASSION AND LOVE FOR THE PEOPLE, WE WILL ALWAYS SEE GOD PUT HIS BLESSING ON IT, WHICH WILL RESULT IN A SUPERNATURAL DISPLAY OF GOD'S POWER.**

Matthew 15:32-37 (NKJV)
"Now Jesus called His disciples to Himself and said, 'I have compassion on the multitude, because they have now continued with Me three days and have nothing to eat. And I do not want to send them away hungry, lest they faint on the way.' 33 Then His disciples said to Him, 'Where could we get enough bread in the wilderness to fill such a great multitude?' 34 Jesus said to them, 'How many loaves do you have?' And they said, 'Seven, and a few little fish.' 35 So He commanded the multitude to sit down on the ground. 36 And He took the seven loaves and the fish and gave thanks, broke them and gave them to His

disciples; and the disciples gave to the multitude. 37 So they all ate and were filled, and they took up seven large baskets full of the fragments that were left."

Without compassion and love being our highest motive to serve the people, we will not experience supernatural multiplication. Multiplication is another word for growth! The enemy of our faith understands this spiritual principle, so he does everything that he can to overtake our love walk. Could it be, the reason we are not seeing more of the supernatural in our lives and ministries is because our love walk has been conquered? We must be aware of the spiritual warfare that seems to always be present especially when we are getting ready to carry out a ministry assignment. We cannot let anything, anyone or any situation conquer our love. If the enemy conquers our love, he has conquered the effectiveness of our ministry and we will not see the supernatural multiplication and power of God touch anyone's life. It's no coincidence that right before we are ready to go to church or do a work of God, that arguments, division, opportunities to be offended surround us. The enemy has a clear strategy to strip us of our love, joy and power. He strips us, every time we choose to hold onto to a grudge, refuse to forgive, or stay angry. When we show up to do ministry, without love, we are also showing up with no power to transform lives. The fact is that a church that has no love, is spiritually dead and will not see growth; nothing that is dead grows. It's that serious! A church or organization without love is just a secular organization with secular programs that will not impact souls for eternity.

> **WHEN WE SHOW UP TO DO MINISTRY, WITHOUT LOVE, WE ARE ALSO SHOWING UP WITH NO POWER TO TRANSFORM LIVES.**

The Good news is that we choose what kind of atmosphere we are going to have in our homes, churches and businesses. ***If we choose to create an atmosphere of love, we will see multiplication, increase, and growth.*** In this chapter we have discovered the most important spiritual principle of Guaranteed Growth and that is creating an atmosphere of love. This will not be easy, but it will sure be worthwhile, especially when we see the results.

Now that we have learned how to build an atmosphere of love, it's time to grow!!

COMMITMENT TO GROW

Name:

Organization:

Signature:

Date:

COMMITMENT TO GROW

CHAPTER 2

ACTION PLAN

FOR CREATING AN ATMOSPHERE OF LOVE

LIST 5 THINGS YOU CAN APPLY FROM THIS CHAPTER
TO EXPERIENCE GUARANTEED GROWTH

#1

#2

#3

#4

#5

CHAPTER THREE

PRINCIPLE #2 "DOING WHAT GOD HAS CALED US TO DO LEADS TO GUARANTEED GROWTH"

CHAPTER 3

PRINCIPLE #2 – DOING WHAT GOD HAS CALLED US TO DO LEADS TO GUARANTEED GROWTH

One of the major reasons we have experienced growth in the last 16 years is our focus on what God has called us to do. God has given us a clear vision of where and with who we are to expand our efforts. God has called us to the inner cities of the United States and eventually the world. We are called to reach out to the broken and hurting in our inner cities. If it's not inner city ministry we don't get involved in it. This type of clarity allows us to only say yes to what God has blessed us to do. Once we identified our where and who, we made a vision statement that the whole church could read and memorize. This vision statement keeps us on track.

OUR VISION STATEMENT

"Bringing Salvation to the INNER CITIES of the world, through the preaching of the Gospel, loving people, meeting their needs, making disciples of Jesus Christ

and developing leaders who build the local church that transforms the community.

God has a specific assignment for every ministry in the world. Once we discover it, we have discovered our growth zone. The growth and increase we have all been looking for is found in our assignment.

The purpose of this chapter is to help us identify our specific call and assignment. When we have identified our God given assignment, we will also discover our growth destination. Our growth destination is the place that God has created and anointed us to experience growth and success. Every church organization, business and ministry must hear from God and discover what they are specifically called to do. Until we identify our God given assignment, we will experience nothing but frustration and disappointment. We will be like a ship tossed and driven by the wind that cannot arrive at its destination.

> **UNTIL WE IDENTIFY OUR GOD GIVEN ASSIGNMENT, WE WILL EXPERIENCE NOTHING BUT FRUSTRATION AND DISAPPOINTMENT.**

We can learn a lesson from the secular business world. In order for a business to succeed it must first create a business plan that describes the specific goods and services that they will provide and specific target group that they are aiming at.

Let's play a game of word association to drive this point a little further. When we hear;

- "Good Year" - What is the first thing we think of?... Of course tires!
- "Chick-fil-A" = Chicken Sandwiches
- "Apple"= Phones and computers
- "Dodgers" = Baseball

Each one of these businesses succeeded only after they were clear about what goods and services they were going to provide and who was their specific target group. No business or organization can succeed trying to reach everybody and do everything.

If we were to ask the majority of churches and ministries who they are called to reach they would most likely say the whole world. That answer sounds right, but until we identify a specific part of the world or group of people we are specifically called to reach. We are basically shooting an arrow with no bulls-eye.

Jesus gave the apostles a promise of the Holy Spirit, but with the promise he also gave them a specific starting point, Jerusalem. If the apostles didn't start in Jerusalem, they would have never seen the supernatural growth that they experienced. Not only do we need to know that we are called, but also know to who, where and to what we are called.

Acts 1:8 (NKJV)
But you shall receive power when the Holy Spirit has come upon you;
and you shall be witnesses to Me in Jerusalem, and in all Judea and Samaria, and to the end of the earth."

With every call there are specific instructions. All of us have a part to play in the big scheme of things. Many organizations and ministries can't grow, because they don't know what part of the body they are, so by default they begin to mimic other parts of the body that are succeeding and as a result fail miserably. Yes, we are all part of the overall body of Christ, but no one church or organization is called to do and be the whole body. God has put each part of the body where He wants it, to do what he wants it to do.

1 Corinthians 12:18 (NLT)
But our bodies have many parts, and God has put each part just where he wants it. 19 How strange a body would be if it had only one part! 20 Yes, there are many parts, but only one body. 21 The eye can never say to the hand, "I don't need you."
The head can't say to the feet, "I don't need you."

If a foot is trying to be an eye it will fail. No matter how hard it works the foot is not equipped to see and will never succeed at it. A major reason why many ministries don't grow is that they have not identified who they are and who they are called to reach. We will never succeed or grow if we are trying to do everything, reach everyone, and do it everywhere. We will only experience supernatural growth when we do what we were created to do in the way he created us to do it. In the next chapter, we will focus on discovering our specific call as a church or organization by reviewing, "Six Facts About Growth Related To Our Calling."

CHAPTER FOUR
HOW TO BUILD PRINCIPLE #2
SIX FACTS THAT WILL HELP US IDENTIFY OUR CALLING

CHAPTER 4

HOW TO BUILD PRINCIPLE #2

SIX FACTS ABOUT GROWTH RELATED TO OUR CALLING

FACT #1 - GOD ALWAYS CALLS US TO A SPECIFIC GEOGRAPHICAL AREA

This specific area is our "growth destination." God has a specific geographical area or group of people he has called us to. For example, we might feel a strong call to take care of orphans throughout the world, but for us to be effective we would have to narrow it down to a specific geographical area and then identify what specific orphans we are going to concentrate our efforts on. All of us need to have a geographical starting point.

MY STORY

I as a Pastor was specifically called to the city of San Bernardino. I personally would have never chosen San Bernardino as my growth destination, because it was a place where nothing was growing. San Bernardino was the least likely place to start a church. After doing some research, I found out that 9 out of 10 churches were shut down after a year of doing ministry in this city. San Bernardino was a place with a disastrous combination of great poverty and limited resources to meet the needs. Not only were the people in poverty, but so was the city. The city filed bankruptcy and is still in bankruptcy proceedings to this date. God's growth destination for us has nothing to do with the conditions or our probability of success. Supernatural growth will always follow radical obedience to go where God calls us to go. God told Abraham to go to a specific place that He would show him and in that place God promised to supernaturally bless Him.

SUPERNATURAL GROWTH WILL ALWAYS FOLLOW RADICAL OBEDIENCE TO GO WHERE GOD CALLS US TO GO.

Genesis 12:1 (NKJV)
Now the Lord had said to Abram:
"Get out of your country,
From your family and from your father's house,
to a land that I will show you.
2 I will make you a great nation; I will bless you
and make your name great; And you shall
be a blessing.

If Abraham would have stayed where he was, he would have never seen the vision come to pass. One of the greatest discoveries we can make is to find out "where" God wants us to do ministry or business. Even though I was called to be a Pastor, I was not called to be a Pastor for every city. There was a specific city and people He called me to. Could it be that we are not experiencing growth because we are trying to reach a city or a group of people we are not called to? A great example of this is Jonah. Jonah was called to go to the city of Nineveh, but he took a ship to Tarsus. As long as Jonah was running from his growth destination he would be frustrated and not see the results of his calling as a prophet of God.

Question: Where has God called you to do ministry or business? Let's be as specific as possible. You should start with a nation, then a city, and eventually a physical address.

FACT #2 - OUR PASSION WILL LEAD US TO OUR CALLING

God will give us passion for what he has called us to do. We can't do ministry through guilt trips. We must not feel bad if we don't have any deep passion to do missionary work in Africa. It doesn't mean that we are ungodly, it just means that we won't be selling everything we own and moving to Africa to start a mission.

There are parts of the body that are supposed to do that. What we are passionate about will not always be what others are passionate about. God has given each one of us a specific work to do.

When we are led by the passion that God has placed in our heart, it will not end in frustration. The passion we have for what we are called to do and the people we are called to reach will get us through the difficult times. Getting through the difficult times is a major key to success and growth.

> **WHEN WE ARE LED BY THE PASSION THAT GOD HAS PLACED IN OUR HEART, IT WILL NOT END IN FRUSTRATION.**

The greatest advice that can be given to someone that desires to start a ministry, career or business, is to pursue what they are passionate and gifted to do. Passion will always lead to success, prosperity and increase. If we are in a field or ministry work that we have no passion for, we will never see growth because we will quit before the breakthrough. It is our love for the people we are serving and purpose we are fulfilling that will give us the perseverance that will lead us to Guaranteed Growth and success.

Good News: All of us have an inward compass that will point us in the right direction towards growth and prosperity, and that's the passion and desires He has put in our heart. First passion and delight come, then comes fulfillment. God promises to give us the desires or passions of our heart.

> *Psalm 37:4 (NIV)*
> *Take delight in the Lord, and he will give you*
> *the desires of your heart.*

Question: Who or what group of people do you have a passion to reach and help relieve their pain?

God will never give us a call or vision without a passion to reach out to a specific group of people. Remember a God vision is all about people. If we can identify this group, we have just identified our growth zone. These are the people we will be the most effective with and experience the greatest joy in serving. We will be most effective with this group because before time began God assigned them to us and us to them. Once we have identified the people we are called to reach, we become a human magnet. When people hear the passionate vision that comes from our heart for them, it will resonate in their heart and will cause them to be drawn to us as well. God gives us passion for this specific group of people so that we can love and develop them.

REMEMBER A GOD VISION IS ALL ABOUT PEOPLE.

John 18:9 (NKJV)
That the saying might be fulfilled which He spoke,
"Of those whom You gave Me I have lost none."

Is it a city, is it a nationality, is it children, is it women, is it senior citizens, is it the homeless, prisoners, girls that are being sex trafficked? Is it the education field, health industry, finances, construction, business, food or entertainment industry that we feel a deep passion for? We need to know which segment of society or need that we are focusing on meeting. Jesus knew to whom he was called - the lost sheep of Israel. He catered his whole ministry to reaching this specific group.

Matthew 15:24 (NIV)
He answered, "I was sent only to the
lost sheep of Israel."

This principle of being led by passion will always lead us to Guaranteed Growth.

MY "PASSION" STORY

There have been two major passions in my life, and they have both led to massive success and growth.

The first passion I discovered was cars. I have always loved cars since I was a little boy. When I was small, I had hundreds of Hot Wheels miniature cars that I would play with all day, sometimes for 8 hours a day. Years later, as an adult, this passion would lead me to a 14-year career in the car business. When I was struggling with what career path I should take, I asked myself: "What can I do?" and as soon I asked that question, my passion spoke up loud and clear - cars!! You love cars! Why not start a career in the car business?" That was one of the best decisions I ever made in my life. That passion for cars led me to a career that I enjoyed and as a result I was able to support my family and be a blessing to my church financially for those 14 years. Throughout my career, I received promotion after promotion because I was letting my passion lead me.

Our God has given all of us a passion for something or some group. Following that God-given passion is guaranteed to lead us to growth and advancement. One universal character trait of the successful: they are passionate.

> **OUR GOD HAS GIVEN ALL OF US A PASSION FOR SOMETHING.**

The second passion that God put in my heart was people. I have always had a heart for people, especially the hurting and forgotten in the broken inner cities of America and the world. This passion led me to start a church. Today, this ministry is touching thousands of people every week. I love what I do!

I will never forget the night that I knew I was called to start a church. God gave me a dream and told me, "Go! There are sheep and you are their shepherd and if you don't go they won't have a shepherd." That was the first time I ever heard the concept that there were specific people assigned to me and I to them. Though I did not know all of them personally yet, they were waiting for my response to the call. All I needed to do was accept the call, and then God would begin to release people that were passionate about what I was passionate about.

The following night, I had another dream and I saw huge trees that were knocked down with massive root systems. I asked God, "What does this mean?" and he responded "These are my ministers that have been hurt in ministry and if you don't respond to the call, they will never be planted and bear fruit again." I began to realize the awesome responsibility that was being placed on my shoulders. Not only were people's eternal lives at stake, but also their God-given purpose. It was all dependent on my response to God's call. I could see God already had a growth plan. My responsibility was to walk it out and let God continually add the workers and the sheep on a daily basis. To this day, the passion that God has given me for His people continues to lead me to increase and growth. I am really excited for the next season of growth and expansion. This excitement is founded on the passion that's in my heart for His people. Where there is passion, there will be growth.

> **WHERE THERE IS PASSION, THERE WILL BE GROWTH.**

FACT #3 - GROWTH BEGINS WHEN WE ACCEPT THE CALL AND BEGIN SHARING IT WITH OTHERS.

MY STORY

The first person I shared God's vision and call for my life with was my wife. I told her, "It looks like God is calling us to start a church". She responded, "Where and how?". I told her I did not know where and I did not know how, but I knew that I had been called. Once I accepted the call, God began to lead us because it was His vision. He began to fill in the blanks. As long as we followed His lead, he would make sure the vision would come to pass.

Habakkuk 2:2-3 (ESV)
And the Lord answered me: "Write the vision; make it plain on tablets, so he may run who reads it. 3 For still the vision awaits its appointed time; it hastens to the end—it will not lie. If it seems slow, wait for it, it will surely come; it will not delay.

AS I BEGAN TO SHARE THE VISION, THE WORKERS SHOWED UP.

As I began to share the vision, the workers showed up. Habakkuk 2:2 says... we should write the vision and make it as plain as possible so that men may run with it. There were people already assigned to run with this ministry, they only needed to hear it and they knew that this was their call. I did not have to coerce people to follow. God had already prepared their hearts for this moment. They began to say "This is exactly what I have been looking for my whole life!" That's why it's so important to get a vision from God and share it, because in God's vision, there is always success and increase!

FACT #4 - A CALL WILL ONLY COME TO PASS IF WE ARE WILLING TO LEAVE OUR COMFORT

If you are going to see growth and increase you have never seen, you will have to be willing to do and go to places you have never been.

We must trust God, because he is always leading us to increase. He's always leading us to more. He's always leading us to a higher level. We cannot wait for perfect conditions or a totally mapped out plan, before we begin to take action on the call on our lives.

> **WE CANNOT WAIT FOR PERFECT CONDITIONS OR A TOTALLY MAPPED OUT PLAN, BEFORE WE BEGIN TO TAKE ACTION ON THE CALL ON OUR LIVES.**

MY STORY

Right after I shared the vision with my wife, a job opportunity came up that would relocate me to the city of San Bernardino. I discussed this job opportunity with my wife and we agreed it was a something we should pursue. In order for the call to be fulfilled, I needed to be willing for God to change my surroundings and get me out of my comfort zone. In every call, there must be steps of faith.

Within the first week of being in San Bernardino, I asked my wife to meet me after work. We drove around the city to make sure that this was the place God was calling us to start the church. As we began to drive around the city, we felt God confirm that this was the place. We saw all the hurt, the pain, the poverty, homeless people on the streets, gangs, prostitutes, heavy drug abuse and broken homes. We knew that this would be a place where Jesus would be saving those who were lost and broken. It was like a homing device. God was leading us to a specific area of the town. We stopped and I asked my wife, "what do you think?" She told me "I believe this is it." I told her "I do too." That was the starting point of The Way World Outreach Ministries. Saying yes at that moment was easy, but I didn't know what God would ask of me right after my acceptance. He told me to move into the very city He was calling me to. Moving into San Bernardino would mean that I would have to sell my dream home that I had just built and move into a city that was crime-ridden and gang-infested. It wasn't just me moving into this city, I was bringing my five girls into a struggling school district. It takes faith to be all in and be willing to follow God's lead out of our comfort zone, but when we are out of our comfort zone we are in our growth zone!

> **WHEN WE ARE OUT OF OUR COMFORT ZONE WE ARE IN OUR GROWTH ZONE!**

FACT #5 - WE FULFILL THE CALL BY HEARING THE VOICE OF GOD

MY STORY

Now that I knew where we would start the church, I still did not know how it would be done. I had never started a church, so I had to depend on hearing the voice of God.

It is important for us to hear God's voice because His Word will never return void it will always accomplish what He has sent it out to do.

> *Isaiah 55:11 (NKJV)*
> *So shall My word be that goes forth from My mouth; It shall not return to Me void, But it shall accomplish what I please, And it shall prosper in the thing for which I sent it.*

All God needs to accomplish His will on earth is for us to hear His voice and follow His lead. In order for us to hear the voice of God, we have to start a new habit of setting time aside on a daily basis in prayer with a pen and paper and asking Him for a download.

One important thing to note is that God will not give us new instructions if we have been unfaithful in carrying out the last instructions He has given us.

We must depend on hearing the voice of God. It must become a lifestyle, because God never reveals the whole vision and plan in one moment. Thank God that He has given us the Holy Spirit to lead us to all truth. We don't need to figure out everything, God has it already figured out. Our responsibility is to ask and we will receive.

James 1:5 (ESV)
If any of you lacks wisdom, let him ask God, who gives generously to all without reproach, and it will be given him.

Anytime and anywhere a man or a woman hear and do His Word, there will be growth and progress. We are one Word away from our next level of growth. Our part is to remain teachable and humble, always realizing that we don't know how. Without consistently hearing the voice of God, we will never succeed and see His growth plan developed in our lives and ministries.

> **WE ARE ONE WORD AWAY FROM OUR NEXT LEVEL OF GROWTH.**

FACT #6 - WE DO WHAT WE CAN AND GOD WILL DO WHAT WE CAN'T

MY STORY

I now had to seek, knock, and ask with a persistent resolution on what were the next steps. (Matthew 7:7)

God responded with instructions. These were His instructions. He wanted us to start a church without a building by going to the toughest, crime-ridden neighborhoods we could find and knock on their doors. This was really out of my comfort zone. I heard about people in the church knocking on doors, but I had never known anyone who actually did it. These instructions would change my life forever. It all sounded ridiculous at the time. I found out that the instructions wouldn't always make sense or be something that I would necessarily want to do, but if I did what I could, God would do what I couldn't.

A great example of this principle in action was a man named Naaman. He was a general in the army of Syria, but he had leprosy, which was a fatal disease. He eventually went to see Elijah, a Prophet of God for healing. To his surprise, Elijah didn't even answer the door. He just gave him instructions to dip in the Jordan river seven times, and promised he would be healed. All Naaman had to do was what he could, and

God would do what he couldn't. To make a long story short, Naaman, after a brief twisting of his arm, finally went to the dirty Jordan river and dipped in it seven times and was instantly healed. Wow! God can do what we *can't do* when we do what we *can do*! The miracle of growth is God's part, the planting of seeds and watering is our part. We do the possible and He does the impossible.

Going back to my story, a small team of inexperienced people and I knocked on doors and God did what we couldn't. He touched their hearts and transformed their lives. Many of those first doors we knocked on and the people we met became members of our church and are still part of our church today. To drive the point a little further, we pray for the sick and God heals them. We preach the Gospel and the Holy Spirit convicts them and saves them. We show up and God does the miracles. Our part is the possible, God's part is the impossible.

We have seen amazing growth in these last 16 years just because we know we have heard from God and have been faithful to the people He has called us to reach.

QUESTIONS:

1. *Who and where has God called you to reach?*

NOTE: God has given each one of us a passion for a specific group of people. All we have to do is accept the call and we will see the growth and increase we have all been looking for. Within every one of us there is a desire for more and God has put that desire in our heart.

2. *Who and what are you passionate about?*

NOTE: The passion God has put in your heart will lead you to your calling.

3. *Are you spending time with God with the specific purpose of hearing His voice?*

4. *What instructions has God given you in relation to the call on your life?*

NOTE: Remember we do the possible and God the impossible.

CHAPTER FIVE

PRINCIPLE #3 *"A CHURCH THAT FINDS AND MEETS NEEDS IS GUARANTEED TO GROW"*

CHAPTER 5

PRINCIPLE #3 – A CHURCH THAT FINDS AND MEETS NEEDS IS GUARANTEED TO GROW!

Any church or organization that is finding and meeting the needs of the church and community is guaranteed to grow!

> *Titus 3:14 (NLT)*
> *"Our people must learn to do good by meeting the urgent needs of others; then they will not be unproductive."*

Growth is not luck! It's intentional with guaranteed spiritual laws, that if applied, will produce consistent growth. As we dive into this chapter, we will discover a principle that leads to Guaranteed Growth. The pattern is simple, find a need and meet it. Jesus practiced this principle in His ministry. In His first miracle, He turned the water into wine. His mother discovered a need; the wedding party ran out of wine so she brought the need to Jesus to meet it. We will continue to see this principle practiced throughout the New Testament, people discovering needs and bringing them to Jesus to meet them. Every time a need was met, massive growth and multiplication would follow. Huge crowds would begin to follow Jesus because they knew He was the source of meeting their needs, whether it was healing, hope, love, freedom, or feeding them when they were hungry.

We continue to practice this principle every time we find a need and meet it through the resources, love, and the Spirit of God in our lives. Meeting needs must be a driving force in any ministry organization that expects to grow and be effective.

> **MEETING NEEDS MUST BE A DRIVING FORCE IN ANY MINISTRY ORGANIZATION THAT EXPECTS TO GROW AND BE EFFECTIVE.**

The business world already knows and practices this principle. They call it a niche. Once they find that need and meet it, they now have prosperity. Let me re-emphasize that, the need is attached to our prosperity, so when we find a need, we just found our vein of growth. So let's start digging! We cannot wait for people to come knocking at our doors, especially if we don't have anything that they need. A church or organization that does not meet needs, will simply not grow.

Let's do whatever it takes to get connected to the people that we have been assigned to serve and find out what their needs are and develop ministries to meet those needs. If we need to do surveys, knock on doors, do research, ask questions. By all means necessary, let's find out what the needs are. If this question is not answered, our church cannot be fruitful.

OUR JOURNEY

Our journey to find the needs began by stepping onto the dangerous streets of the city of San Bernardino and meeting the people we were called to serve. After spending three months talking to people on the streets of San Bernardino, we were ready to create a plan of action to serve our community that would lead to Guaranteed Growth. The foundational story of our church is filled with stories of how discovering the needs of our community gave us the clarity we needed to unlock the hearts of the people so that we could effectively serve them.

OUR STORY

It was a hot summer day when my brother and I stepped out onto the streets of San Bernardino in one of the toughest areas in town to start meeting people. The truth of the matter was that I was a little bit uncomfortable with the instructions God had given me. He had instructed me to go where the people were and knock on their doors with the purpose of loving them by discovering their needs and meeting them. Not only was I intimidated about knocking on doors, I knew that in every hood there was always a vicious pit-bull dog running loose. I found myself asking God the same question Jesus asked, "Is there any other way?" After wrestling with God, I finally gave in and continued to move forward with the instructions that God gave me to go knock on doors. But I still had another question: "What am I going to say when I knock on the door?" God answered, "The purpose of knocking on the door is to find out what the needs are in the community so that you can meet them." The second purpose was to build loving relationships with the people.

If the church does not meet the needs of the community and develop meaningful relationships, it will not have the influence to transform lives. If we can get the people to give us permission to serve them, by meeting their needs, we can also get permission to lead them. Our main goal is to lead them into a loving relationship with Jesus Christ and His church. Every time the cycle of finding needs, meeting needs and leading them to Jesus is completed, disciples of Jesus Christ are created and the church grows. After all, this is the essence of all church growth.

> **IF THE CHURCH DOES NOT MEET THE NEEDS OF THE COMMUNITY AND DEVELOP MEANINGFUL RELATIONSHIPS, IT WILL NOT HAVE THE INFLUENCE TO TRANSFORM LIVES.**

The first thing we did before we knocked on the door was to do a prayer walk around the block. I don't know if I was being extra spiritual or just procrastinating. In every pivotal moment of growth, there will be times where our faith will be tested and either we let fear take over and back out or move forward in faith under the leadership of the Holy Spirit. We must remember that God is with us and He will help us succeed. God will never take us to a place of defeat or loss.

After our prayer walk, it was time to take action and knock on our first door. This would be our first contact with someone in the neighborhood that God had called us to reach. As the pastor of the church, I knew this was the perfect time to delegate my authority. I asked my brother to knock on the first door and I would be on the lookout for the pit-bulls. Once I saw the coast was clear, I joined my brother at the door and we introduced ourselves. This was our first step to building a church that would impact the whole world. We told our first person that came to answer the door that we were thinking about starting a church in San Bernardino, but before we did we wanted to find out what the needs were in the community, so we could better serve them. Her request was very simple, she just wanted prayer for her son that was struggling with an issue. We prayed with her and she was so grateful that someone would go out of their way and be there for her in her time of need. I realized knocking on doors wasn't as bad as I thought it was going to be. We actually made a friend at that door and today she has been a member of our church for the last sixteen years. Growth was already happening at the first door we knocked on. God was confirming that if we would follow His lead, He would always bless the ministry with increase. This is exactly how Jesus did ministry, walking in the highways and byways meeting the needs of the broken and hurting in their time of distress. The Bible tells us clearly that we are to go and preach the Gospel. The key word is "go." We are to go out of our way, go into the neighborhood, and go specifically to find a need and meet it. That's what true love is…finding someone's greatest need and sacrificially doing everything we can to meet that need without expecting anything in return. We continued to knock on doors with a pure heart, with the motive to love people right where they were. Since we had no church to invite them to and no place to meet, our church was now on the front porch of the doors that God sent us to. Behind every one of these doors, there was a soul that God was so desperately longing to have a relationship with. I now understand why God wanted us to start on the streets. We can become so comfortable within the four walls of our church buildings that we forget that our mission is to reach out to the lost right where they are. Our ministries will never grow unless we intentionally go out and find needs and meet them.

> **THAT'S WHAT TRUE LOVE IS... FINDING SOMEONE'S GREATEST NEED AND SACRIFICIALLY DOING EVERYTHING WE CAN TO MEET THAT NEED.**

After that first day of knocking on doors, we were on our way to the next step. We began to take over the neighborhood one block at a time. We got to the point that we adopted twelve blocks with teams of two visiting each of the blocks consistently every week. God not only gave us a vision to adopt blocks, he sent us great people to help us carry out the assignment.

CHAPTER SIX
HOW TO BUILD PRINCIPLE #3
TWO INSIGHTS TO EFFECTIVELY MEETING NEEDS

CHAPTER 6

HOW TO BUILD PRINCIPLE #3

TWO INSIGHTS TO EFFECTIVELY MEETING NEEDS

GROWTH INSIGHT #1

God will always send us the amount of people we need to fulfill the vision he has given us.

Our goal was to love the people, meet their needs, and develop relationships with each of the families we came into contact with. We began to find out how deep the pain, suffering, and poverty was in our city. Behind these doors, we found families that did not have any food and did not know where their next meal was coming from. This was a time when they needed more than just a prayer. They needed to see our faith in action. James 2:15 (NLT) exhorts us that, "If we find a brother or sister with no food and say good bye and have a good day and don't feed them, our faith is dead." Faith without a corresponding action will never save anyone, and therefore will not produce kingdom growth. We knew it was time for us to go to the grocery store and buy groceries and bring it to them. Who bought the groceries? We did. It was time to invest in the people we were called to reach. By feeding them, we were feeding Jesus. Matthew 25:35 says, "When I was hungry you fed me."

We continued to feed the hungry week after week. Unknowingly, we were planting seeds into our future food ministry. Everything we do for the Lord is never in vain, it will always produce a harvest. Today, we are one of the top food pantries in Southern California. We distribute over 1 million pounds of food every year to the hungry in our community. How does that happen in a city that is impoverished? It is through one of the most important principles that Jesus exemplified.

GROWTH INSIGHT #2

Anytime God shows you a need, he will give you the supernatural ability to meet that need.

The disciples were struggling with that same issue when he told them to feed the 5,000. They asked in Mark 8:4, "'How are we supposed to find enough food to feed them here in the wilderness?' And Jesus asked 'how much bread do you have?'" Jesus already had the provision matched up with the need. All the disciples needed to do was to use what they had and God would bring the multiplication. This is always how it works. Every need is an opportunity for ministry and growth. That's why we need to be careful that we are not shying away from the need. Instead we must ask God to help us meet that need. If we are shying away from the need, we are running away from growth and our destiny.

> **EVERY NEED IS AN OPPORTUNITY FOR MINISTRY AND GROWTH.**

We continued this process of finding needs and meeting them. We found homes that did not have a stove or fridge, with children eating out of an ice chest. We immediately knew the thing to do. It was time to go and buy a fridge and a stove and bring it to them. We found senior citizens who needed assistance. Their homes and their lawns were un-kept, because they no longer had the strength to do it themselves. We would send teams to mow their lawns, clean their house, and if needed, paint their homes. Not only did we find physical needs, but also spiritual needs. We found families who had just lost their loved ones through gang violence and were going through one of the toughest times of their lives. We were able to love them, comfort them, and give them spiritual direction in their time of crisis. We also knocked on a door and found out that a 15-year old girl had just committed suicide by hanging herself from the rafters in her own living room. To help them recover, we knew we had to do more. We installed drywall to cover the rafters and gave their living room a make-over. This way they would no longer have to see the image of their daughter hanging there. If we had never gone to the streets, we would have never been able to minister and love these people that were in such desperate need for Jesus Christ to save them.

As we continued knocking on doors, we met up with people from all walks of life. They all had the same thing in common: a need that we could meet through the love of Christ. We met up with children, teenagers, the disabled, drug dealers, gang members, alcoholics, single moms with husbands in prison, doing everything they could just to survive. The words of Christ were echoing in my mind that "The harvest is ripe and the laborers are few" (Luke 10:2). It was so easy to get overwhelmed with all the needs that we were finding. Today, the church is needed more than ever.

The next level of church growth is all around us. We need to ask God to open our eyes and renew our passion for the lost and the hurting. I remember one day, when I went out with my five daughters to minister to the block that was assigned to us. It took us around two hours, in the hot sun, to knock on all the doors. After we were done, we got into the car and began to drive home. I looked to the right and I saw a park in the neighborhood, full of what looked like a large group of homeless people. I told my daughters that we were going to make one more stop. We all got out of the car and began to approach the crowd. One of the men came up to me, I introduced myself and I told him that we were thinking about starting a church in this area. I wanted to find out what their needs were. He told me that they were hungry and that most of them had not eaten all day, because there was no feeding program on Saturday. I drove off with my daughters and went to a local fast food restaurant and got as many #1 combos that I could (burrito, fries, and a coke). I came back with my daughters and we distributed those meals to the homeless in that park. That day was the beginning of our ministry to reach out to the homeless.

THE NEXT LEVEL OF CHURCH GROWTH IS ALL AROUND US.

Today we have a ministry called "The Way Out" that reaches out to the homeless. It meets their needs and is able to get every one of them off the streets and to rebuild their lives. Every need that we found was creating growth in our church. One of the major ways that God brings increase is through ministry expansion. So when we discover a need and take ownership of it, we have just discovered a ministry that will bring Guaranteed Growth to the church. With every ministry that is created, God will send people that he has assigned to those ministries to volunteer, support and lead.

> **WITH EVERY MINISTRY THAT IS CREATED, GOD WILL SEND PEOPLE THAT HE HAS ASSIGNED TO THOSE MINISTRIES TO VOLUNTEER, SUPPORT AND LEAD.**

After two months of consistently visiting these homes and walking these streets, people began to ask us where our church was. We would respond, "We don't have a church, but when we do, will you come?" and everyone began to say, "Yes." God finally released us to get a building in the middle of this tough neighborhood. It was a community center that we could use on Sunday mornings and Thursday nights for discipleship. We created a flyer and invited everyone to come. Our grand opening service would start at 10:30am on Sunday morning. God told us to prepare for 500 people to come. It was a lofty goal, but after all, God was involved in this and growth was already part of the plan. God had given us the faith and the strategy to expect supernatural growth. Now that we knew the needs, we could cater our worship service to reach the people that God had called us to reach. We had some of the ladies prepare pots of rice and beans and we went to the local supermarket to buy as much fried chicken as we could. We let all the homeless people know that we would serve food at our grand opening service, and they could invite their friends. This would be a place where they would be welcomed and cared for. I asked all of our volunteers to bring as much clothes as they could, especially children's clothes. The school year would soon begin and many of the children did not have clothes.

On our grand opening day, God's principle of Guaranteed Growth would be put to the test. For two months, we knocked on doors, met needs, built relationships and now it was time for God to bring the increase. By 9:00am we had everything set up, but there was not a soul in sight. As I was waiting outside to welcome our guests, another half hour went by and still no one had arrived. I began to wonder - did we miss it? But right around 10:00 o'clock, I saw people walking from the neighborhoods towards our building. Many of them were going into church for the first time in their lives. What a celebration this was going to be! Over five-hundred people showed up for our first service and hundreds of them were born again and confessed Jesus as Lord. This was one of the biggest days in the history of San Bernardino. It happened through practicing a principle that brings Guaranteed Growth to any church or ministry—Any church or organization that is meeting needs is guaranteed to grow.

Sixteen years later, we are still practicing this principle and seeing God continue to bring growth. We now have fourteen services a week, over one-hundred active ministries, two campuses, and over 7,000 people in weekly attendance. One of our campuses is a Downtown Mission where we help over 10,000 people a month with food, clothes, shelter, and assistance. In this ministry, we have seen thousands of people be born again and lives transformed for eternity. This principle will work everywhere. Growth is not an accident. All we need to do is allow God to use us to continue to find needs and meet them. The next principle that we will discover is the principle of reaching out to the poor and achieving Guaranteed Growth. This principle is closely related to the truth we have just discussed of meeting needs. Let's continue our journey of guaranteed growth.

EXERCISE: Get together with your ministry team and discover the top three needs of your community and create a strategy to meet them.

CHAPTER 6

ACTION PLAN

FOR FINDING NEEDS AND MEETING THEM

LIST 5 THINGS YOU CAN APPLY FROM THIS CHAPTER TO EXPERIENCE GUARANTEED GROWTH

#1

#2

#3

#4

#5

CHAPTER SEVEN

PRINCIPLE #4 — "A CHURCH THAT TAKES CARE OF THE POOR IS GUARANTEED TO GROW"

CHAPTER 7

PRINCIPLE #4 – A CHURCH THAT TAKES CARE OF THE POOR IS GUARANTEED TO GROW!

Psalm 72:12
*"He will rescue the **poor** when they cry to him; he will **help** the oppressed, who have no one to defend them."*

Our grand opening service was a great success. We saw over five-hundred people attend, and hundreds of people gave their lives to Jesus! What an exciting day! Who were the majority of the people that came? It was the poor. I am sure you're asking, "How are you going to build a church with a bunch of poor people? Who is going to pay the bills and keep the ministry financially stable?" Those are great questions. When opening up a ministry in the inner city or in seriously impoverished areas, this will be a concern because of the tremendous need and limited resources. In San Bernardino, many churches shut down within the first year because of this deadly combination. In this chapter, we are going to discuss some major truths that we can bank on when ministering to the poor that will lead to Guaranteed Growth and prosperity. True growth will not only have souls being saved, but also a supernatural provision for all the needs of the ministry being met. Let's dive into these truths and build healthy ministries with a heart for the poor and experience consistent growth.

> **TRUE GROWTH WILL NOT ONLY HAVE SOULS BEING SAVED, BUT ALSO A SUPERNATURAL PROVISION FOR ALL THE NEEDS OF THE MINISTRY BEING MET.**

TRUTH # 1 – GOD'S TOP PRIORITY IS TO MINISTER TO THE POOR!

1 Samuel 2:8 (NLT)
"He lifts the poor from the dust and the needy from the garbage dump. He sets them among princes, placing them in seats of honor. For all the earth is the Lord's and he has set the world in order."

God is on a rescue mission to save the poor! God is not only interested in meeting their needs, but is also focused on restoring their honor. This is what true ministry is all about, transforming lives through the supernatural power of God. God does not make mistakes.

Every person on earth has immeasurable value to God. When others see trash, God sees a treasure! In the dirty streets of our inner cities, abandoned neighborhoods and mission fields, there is a population of poor people that are waiting to be rescued. Our future leaders, volunteers, and givers are waiting to be rescued behind the garbage dumps of our cities. As much as the poor and helpless are longing to be rescued, God's longing to save them is even deeper.

Psalms 12:5 (NLT)
"The Lord replies, 'I have seen violence done to the helpless, and I have heard the groans of the poor. Now I will rise up to rescue them, as they have longed for me to do.'"

God's rescue team is the church. If the church ignores the cries of the poor, it is ignoring the call of God. Ignoring that call could be the very reason why so many ministries are not growing and experiencing a serious decline. If we are going to see a turn-around in our ministries, we are going to have to make the poor our priority.

IF WE ARE GOING TO SEE A TURN-AROUND IN OUR MINISTRIES, WE ARE GOING TO HAVE TO MAKE THE POOR OUR PRIORITY.

Luke 4:18 (NLT)
"The Spirit of the Lord is upon me,
for he has anointed me to
bring Good News to the poor. He has sent me
to proclaim that captives will be
released, that the blind will see, that the
oppressed will be set free."

Jesus started out His ministry with a clear emphasis on reaching out to the poor. His first statement after being in the wilderness for forty days and overcoming every one of His temptations is found in Luke 4:18 - Jesus states that He was "Anointed to preach the good news to the poor." He could have mentioned any other group, but He prioritized the poor.

Matthew 5:3 (NLT)
"God blesses those who are poor and
realize their need for
him, for the Kingdom of Heaven is theirs."

We see this same exact pattern in the "Sermon on the Mount." Jesus begins one of the most important teachings in scripture with the subject of the poor. I don't think this is a coincidence. Jesus intentionally prioritizes the poor. Since the poor are God's top priority, it should be ours as well. Anytime our priorities are in line with God's, there is no way we can fail! Let's get our focus back on the poor and make room for them in our churches and ministries and see God bring a revival of souls being saved. You may ask yourself why such emphasis on the poor? The answer is in the scripture. They are the ones who realize they need God. No one can be saved until they come to a place of acknowledging their own spiritual poverty and need for God to fill it. The poor are ripe for harvest. The kingdom of heaven belongs to the poor because they are the only ones who will receive it. Who are the poor? The poor are those that are in lack and have a need that they cannot meet. Every person on earth is in spiritual poverty and in need of a savior, but it takes a while for some of us to realize it. The poor have hit rock bottom and are the most likely to receive the help God offers through faith in Jesus Christ and the church.

TRUTH # 2 - WHEN WE TAKE CARE OF THE POOR, WE ARE TAKING CARE OF JESUS!

Matthew 25:35-40 (NLT)
"For I was hungry, and you fed me. I was thirsty, and you gave me a drink. I was a stranger, and you invited me into your home. 36 I was naked, and you gave me clothing. I was sick, and you cared for me. I was in prison, and you visited me. 37 Then these righteous ones will reply, 'Lord, when did we ever see you hungry and feed you? Or thirsty and give you something to drink? 38 Or a stranger and show

you hospitality? Or naked and give you clothing? 39 When did we ever see you sick or in prison and visit you?' 40 And the King will say, 'I tell you the truth, when you did it to one of the least of these my brothers and sisters, you were doing it to me!'"

Jesus identifies with the poor so deeply that He states that, "What we have done to the least of them, we have done to Him." Every time we include the poor, we include Jesus. To exclude the poor would also mean that we are excluding Jesus. Could it be that Jesus is trying to get into our churches and ministries through the poor? A ministry that doesn't reach out to the poor is not ministering to Jesus and will not see kingdom growth. A ministry or individual that can see someone hungry, thirsty, and naked and not be moved to help has lost the heart of God. Without having the right heart towards the least of them, God will not bless us with growth. Why would God send people our way, if we don't want to take care of them?

> **A MINISTRY THAT DOESN'T REACH OUT TO THE POOR IS NOT MINISTERING TO JESUS AND WILL NOT SEE KINGDOM GROWTH.**

THREE IMMEDIATE BENEFITS OF TAKING CARE OF THE POOR!

1. GOD WILL PROMOTE OUR MINISTRY!
He will begin to send the needy our way. No greater promoter than God himself.

2. WORD WILL HIT THE STREETS THAT OUR MINISTRY IS THE PLACE TO GET HELP!
"They will begin to say, 'If you need help, go to that church they will help you.'"

3. GOD WILL BEGIN TO SEND WORKERS AND RESOURCES TO MEET NEEDS.
Not only those that need help will come, but also those that have been called to partner up with the ministry. The resources and needs will finally come together. God will supernaturally provide. It's impossible for us to take care of the poor, without Him taking care of us.

Proverbs 19:17 (NKJV)
"He who has pity on the poor lends to the Lord, And He will pay back what he has given."

TRUTH #3 - OUR ATTITUDE TOWARDS THE POOR WILL DETERMINE WHETHER WE HAVE GUARANTEED SUCCESS OR GUARANTEED FAILURE!

Deuteronomy 15:7-8 (NLT)
"But if there are any poor Israelites in your towns when you arrive in the land the Lord your God is giving you, do not be hard-hearted or tightfisted toward them. 8. Instead, be generous and lend them whatever they need."

In this portion of scripture, there are two different attitudes towards the poor and two different guarantees. One attitude guarantees failure and the other guarantees success in all we do.

ATTITUDE #1 - HARD-HEARTED AND TIGHTFISTED!

The first attitude God warns us about is an attitude of being tightfisted and mean-spirited towards the poor. We need to be careful not to be influenced by this mindset. Those infected by this spirit almost have a prejudice towards the poor. They may say, "Helping the poor is enabling them." They use this statement to justify not helping them. When we are feeding the hungry or helping a homeless person off the streets, we are showing them the love of God. Through this act of love, we are ministering to them. I have seen countless souls give their lives to Jesus as a result of an act of kindness. A refusal to help the poor will make us guilty before God. We are commanded to give to the poor. If we ignore their cries, we will be ignored in our time of need. Ignoring the poor can lead us to two negative guarantees. One—just like the poor are in need, we will also find ourselves in great need. The second negative guarantee is that in our time of need no one will come and rescue us either.

WHEN WE ARE FEEDING THE HUNGRY OR HELPING A HOMELESS PERSON OFF THE STREETS, WE ARE SHOWING THEM THE LOVE OF GOD.

Proverbs 21:13 (NLT)
"Those who shut their ears to the cries of the poor will be ignored in their own time of need."

ATTITUDE #2 - GENEROSITY TOWARDS THE POOR!

Deuteronomy 15:10-11 (NLT)
"Give generously to the poor, not grudgingly, for the Lord your God will bless you in everything you do. There will always be some in the land who are poor.

That is why I am commanding you to share freely with the poor and with other Israelites in need."

If our ministries have an attitude of generosity towards the poor, God promises to bless us. A ministry that takes care of the poor will always have the blessing of the Lord upon them. God will give us His favor in all we do. We can't afford to do ministry without the blessing or favor of God. I have seen this blessing in action in our ministry. With this blessing of the Lord, we have everything we need to do the impossible. In our city we have many children that have never been in church and live in neighborhoods where drug dealing, prostitution, and gang violence constantly surround them. I had a vision to start a bus ministry to bring these children into our local church. The only problem that we faced was that we had no buses or money. Since our goal was to take care of the poor, we were partnering up with God's mission. God came through with a huge blessing! Within a month period of time we had nine commercial buses donated to us by a local ministry. I did not know anyone at that ministry, but God knew them and put in a word for us. This is an example of God blessing us in everything we do. Another recent example was an outreach we did in one of the toughest neighborhoods in our city. We had a vision to give every child in that neighborhood a toy. That very week an organization had around 1,000 brand new toys that they wanted to donate for our outreach. The toys were valued at over $10,000 dollars. We did not have the money, but we did have the blessing of God. We see examples of God's blessing on everything we do daily. As long as we continue to be generous to the poor, we will have the blessing of God on everything we set out to do.

> A MINISTRY THAT TAKES CARE OF THE POOR WILL ALWAYS HAVE THE BLESSING OF THE LORD UPON THEM.

TRUTH # 4 - EVERY CHURCH CAN BE FILLED WITH THE POOR!

Luke 14:13-14 (NLT)
"Instead, invite the poor, the crippled,
the lame, and the blind.
14. Then at the resurrection of the righteous,
God will reward you for inviting those
who could not repay you."

Jesus continues to make the poor His top priority, even when it comes to who we should invite into our homes and churches. It's no coincidence that the poor and the disabled are mentioned over and over. Every time Jesus mentions the poor, He also includes an incentive for all who are willing to minister to them.

CHAPTER EIGHT
HOW TO BUILD PRINCIPLE #4
INVITE THE POOR AND UNLOCK TWO GROWTH RESULTS

CHAPTER 8

HOW TO BUILD PRINCIPLE #4

INVITE THE POOR AND UNLOCK TWO GROWTH RESULTS

There are two things that a church that ministers to the poor will be filled or blessed with!

GROWTH RESULT #1 - A CHURCH THAT INVITES THE POOR WILL BE FILLED WITH GOD'S ETERNAL FAVOR!

All that invite the poor are guaranteed a reward! Anything we do for the poor will never be overlooked by God. Those that include the poor and hurting, will be blessed not only in this life, but will also have a great reward in the kingdom to come. The poor always come with the favor of God on them.

> **THE POOR MAY NOT BE ABLE TO IMMEDIATELY REPAY US, BUT GOD WILL.**

We may not know exactly what that eternal reward will be, but we do know that there will be a special distinction and rank in heaven for all that ministered to the poor. The poor may not be able to immediately repay us, but God will.

We have seen God fill our church with His favor over and over. Since the first day we opened the doors of our church, God has blessed us with everything we have needed to minister to the poor. We may not have a large reserve in our bank accounts, but we have a large amount of God's favor. His favor has given us all the resources that we have needed to minister to his people, including miracle buildings. We started out with a 8,000 sq. ft. building and now we have more than 165,000 sq. ft. of space where we are able to minister to the poor and hurting in our community.

MY STORY

I mentioned earlier that God told me to leave my career in the business world, where I had been working for fourteen years to go into full time ministry. I was at the top of my career when God called me to take that leap of faith. God was asking me to totally trust Him to take care of me, my family, and the church. I would go from making $250,000 a year to what looked like nothing. The church didn't have anything in the bank account, but it was full of the favor of God. We had received this favor from our continual ministry to the poor. I remember the first Wednesday night service after I left my job, we received a miracle offering of over $40,000. It was the biggest offering, we had ever received! At that time, I wasn't aware of anyone in our church who had that kind of money. After investigating, I found out that it had come from a lady that I had never met. She was terminally ill, and told me that God had sent her to our church to give one last offering before she passed on. The poor could not give that offering, but God knew someone who could! That lady specifically mentioned what attracted her to our ministry was that we were taking care of the poor and outcasts in our city. She wanted to leave this world on a high note, giving and ministering to God's top priority—the poor. I believe there are people waiting in the wings, ready to serve and be part of financing God's ministry to the poor. Let's go back to a place where our churches and ministries are full of God's favor by reaching out to the poor in our communities.

GROWTH RESULT #2 - A CHURCH THAT INVITES THE POOR WILL BE FILLED WITH PEOPLE!

Luke 14:21-23 (NLT)
"The servant returned and told his master
what they had

> *said. His master was furious and said,*
> *'Go quickly into the streets and alleys of*
> *the town and invite the poor, the crippled,*
> *the blind, and the lame.' 22.*
> *After the servant had done this, he reported,*
> *'There is still room for more.' 23. So his*
> *master said, 'Go out into the country lanes*
> *and behind the hedges and urge anyone*
> *you find to come, so that the house will be full.'"*

The poor will come if they are invited. If we want our churches filled, all we have to do is invite the poor. They will look at it as an honor to be invited. Jesus wants His house full and He shows us how to do it - invite the poor. The poor will come, because they have needs that they know only God and the church can meet. I believe that every seat and pew in our churches can be filled with the poor. We have seen this to be a fact. Since the grand opening of our church, we have never lacked a crowd. The poor have always come and brought their friends. After opening our second campus, we have seen the same pattern continue. The poor and broken always come when they are invited. We started that service by creating a ministry team that made breakfast for the hungry in our community. The breakfast starts at 8:00am and ends around 8:45am ready for the beginning of our 9:00am service. As a result, over three hundred people come and flow into our service. The church is not only full of souls, but also the presence of God. All of our services on Sunday (9am & 11am & 1pm) and Wednesday night services are full of God's presence. We will continue to open new services, as each are filled. These results can happen in all of our ministries and churches. We need to ask God for a strategy to reach out to the poor. The poor are waiting to be invited and rescued out of the dilapidated streets of our cities, ghettos, underpasses, parks, and behind trash bins. Let's bring them in and fill our churches! In this next chapter, we will be introduced to the next principle for Guaranteed Growth. It has to do with another segment of our society that Jesus highly prioritizes, our children.

> **IF WE WANT OUR CHURCHES FILLED, ALL WE HAVE TO DO IS INVITE THE POOR.**

CHAPTER 8

ACTION PLAN

FOR TAKING CARE OF THE POOR

LIST 5 THINGS YOU CAN APPLY FROM THIS CHAPTER TO EXPERIENCE GUARANTEED GROWTH

#1

#2

#3

#4

#5

CHAPTER NINE

PRINCIPLE #5 — "A CHURCH THAT HAS AN EXCELLENT CHILDREN'S MINISTRY IS GUARANTEED TO GROW"

CHAPTER 9

PRINCIPLE #5 – A CHURCH THAT HAS AN EXCELLENT CHILDREN'S MINISTRY IS GUARANTEED TO GROW!

Our children have never been in such need of love and attention. Ministries and organizations that intentionally focus on children can really make an impact in their communities.

Children's ministry is one of the areas we can focus on with the greatest growth potential. We are living in a society where more and more of our children are feeling the weight of broken families and are exposed to a world with little to no values. The trends in our present world have totally changed. The majority of our children are now coming from broken homes and absentee fathers. In 1960 children that came from a single parent home was only 9% - today 1 in 4 children come from fatherless homes.

CHILDREN'S MINISTRY IS ONE OF THE AREAS WE CAN FOCUS ON WITH THE GREATEST GROWTH POTENTIAL.

These are the hard facts...we must intervene:
63% of youth suicides are from fatherless homes.
90% of all the homeless come from fatherless homes.
71% of all dropouts come from fatherless homes.
And 85% of all youth in prison come from fatherless homes.[2]

Right now, there are more than twenty-four million children without fathers. They desperately need to be connected to their heavenly father and be mentored by the local church.

Another plague that has negatively affected our children is the high level of drug and alcohol abuse. Twenty-three and a half million people, age twelve and older, need treatment for alcohol and drug abuse. The U.S. is experiencing the highest levels of drug addiction in its history. From our everyday experience in ministry, many of our children in our inner cities have parents that are neglecting them because of their destructive addictions. If we do not rescue them, we are letting the enemy continue this cycle of self-destruction. We, as a church, can really make an impact in our cities by intentionally creating ministries that minister to them

---
[2] https://www.liveabout.com/fatherless-children-in-america-statistics-1270392

with great love and excellence. Our children need to be rescued!

In Psalms 72:4 God reminds us to "defend the poor and to rescue the children of the needy."

The third trend that is really disturbing is that seventy percent of the children that grow up in our churches are abandoning their faith when they become young adults. Clearly, we have not done a great job of passing down our faith to the next generation. This trend will continue if we do not drastically change our approach to children's ministry and make it a top priority in our churches. We can't afford to continue to lose our children to the deception of the enemy. The fastest growing religion today is atheism.

It all comes down to lack of training and irrelevant teaching. We must realize that the church, overall, is losing the faith battle because we have not been intentional about making children a top priority. When we make our children and youth ministry a top priority, God will give us creative ideas of how to teach them and make church an exciting place where they can connect with Jesus in a meaningful way. A church that has not prioritized children will continue to lose the next generation and is guaranteed to decline.

I believe it is a sin to have an amazing adult's ministry and have a mediocre children's and youth department. We should make our children's ministry the most exciting place on campus. What's worse than having a mediocre children's department is having no children's ministry at all and making our children sit through our boring adult, age inappropriate services. If we are not willing to make the adjustments, we will continue to lose our children to the world and to the lies of the enemy.

When I talk about a great children's ministry, I'm not speaking about a place of babysitting or childcare. It should be a place of training where their spirits are being enriched with the Word of God in a fun and exciting atmosphere.

Underestimating our children and the importance of a children's ministry, is a crucial mistake. Our children are valuable members of any healthy and growing church.

Now for the good news—If we choose to develop a healthy and vibrant children's ministry, we are guaranteed to experience growth in our ministries! We will be discussing some foundational truths in scripture that guarantee growth, in regards to ministering to children.

FOUR REASONS WHY A GREAT CHILDREN'S MINISTRY WILL CAUSE GUARANTEED GROWTH!

REASON #1 - CHILDREN HAVE GREAT FAITH IN GOD!

Children, when presented with the Gospel, will believe it and be saved. I have never met a child who is an atheist. In order for a child to be an atheist he or she must be taught not to believe. The fact is a substantial majority of the people who accept Jesus Christ as their savior, do so before reaching their eighteenth birthday. Surveys also reveal that young people respond more positively to different outreach influences than do people who embrace Christ later in life. The current Barna study indicates that nearly half of all Americans who accept Jesus Christ as their savior, do so before reaching the age of thirteen (43%), and that two out of three born again Christians (64%) made that commitment to Christ before their eighteenth birthday.

Why wait until they get polluted by the mindset of this world? I believe Satan's greatest strategy is to get the local church to neglect children's ministry and lose our greatest window of opportunity to win them over to Jesus. God promises if we train our children in the way they should go when they are older, we will not lose them.

Proverbs 22:6 (KJV)
Train up a child in the way he should go: and when he is old, he will not depart from it.

This scripture gives us a major insight. The reason that our children are departing is because of lack of training. Our churches and homes should be training centers for our children to follow God. This scripture promises that the intentional training of a child will affect a child's future decisions and core values. God instructs us how to train our children to live for God. The process is simple, we learn the Word of God and diligently teach them to our children. The church should be a place where parents can bring their children to reinforce what they are learning at home.

> **THE CHURCH SHOULD BE A PLACE WHERE PARENTS CAN BRING THEIR CHILDREN TO REINFORCE WHAT THEY ARE LEARNING AT HOME.**

Deuteronomy 6:6-7 (ESV)
And these words that I command you today shall be on your heart. 7 You shall teach them diligently to your children, and shall talk of them when you sit in your house, and when you walk by the way, and when you lie down, and when you rise.

We need to do all we can to effectively reach this generation. God has given all of us influence and access to a multitude of children of which we must take personal responsibility. We only have one shot to reach them and train them while they are children. The good news is that children instinctively believe in Jesus. Let's not be reactive, but proactive. Let's not wait until our children become teens and get brain washed by all the unbelief in this world. It is time for us to realize that the best time to mentor and train them is while they are young. It's not that we can't reach them when they are older, it's just that it will be more difficult. Children already believe in God. Let's reach them in their prime. Jesus gives a look into a child's heart in Matthew 18.

Matthew 18:1-5 (NLT)
"About that time the disciples came to Jesus and asked, 'Who is greatest in the Kingdom of Heaven?' 2 Jesus called a little child to him and
put the child among them. 3 Then he said, 'I tell you the truth, unless you turn
from your sins and become like little children, you will never get into the Kingdom
of Heaven. 4 So anyone who becomes as humble as this little child is the greatest
in the Kingdom of Heaven. 5 And anyone who welcomes a little child like this on
my behalf is welcoming me.'"

Jesus shows us that children have the kind of faith we all need in order to enter into the kingdom of heaven. The greatest harvest in the world is right underneath our nose and that's our children. They are ripe for the harvest. Just like Peter fishing on the wrong side of the boat. Jesus is telling us if we drop our nets, make an effort to reach out to the children, we would see the biggest harvest and growth we have ever seen. Children will be saved, and our churches will grow.

> **THE GREATEST HARVEST IN THE WORLD IS RIGHT UNDERNEATH OUR NOSE AND THAT'S OUR CHILDREN.**

Not only will we grow in numbers, but we will grow in the manifest presence of God. When we welcome the children, we are welcoming Jesus. The opposite conclusion can also be made, if we don't welcome the children, we are not welcoming Jesus into our churches and ministries. Any ministry that takes care of children will see an increase in God's provision and anointing. Everyone wants to partner up with a ministry that is focused on the children, especially parents. A dynamic children's ministry will teach the Gospel and the Word of God to them while their faith is the highest and their learning curve is at its peak. We don't need to let "These little ones who instinctively trust in Jesus to fall into the sin of unbelief."

Jesus taught that it would be better for a person or ministry not to exist if they cause one of His little ones that trust Him to fall into sin, including the sin of unbelief.

Matthew 18:6 (NLT)
"But if you cause one of these little ones who trusts in me to fall into sin, it would be better for you to have a large millstone tied around your neck and be drowned in the depths of the sea."

Let's not be the cause of our children's fall. Let's create a children's ministry that will help build their faith in Christ. He should be the foundation on which they build the rest of their lives.

REASON #2 - PARENTS WANT A PLACE TO BRING THEIR CHILDREN TO JESUS!

Luke 18:15-17 (NLT)
"One day some parents brought their little children to Jesus so he could touch and bless them. But when the disciples saw this, they scolded the parents for bothering him.
16. Then Jesus called for the children and said to the disciples, 'Let the children come to me. Don't stop them! For the Kingdom of God belongs to those who are like these children.
17. I tell you the truth, anyone who doesn't receive the Kingdom of God like a child will never enter it.'"

In this story, we see parents bringing their children to Jesus. Parents are searching for a place where they can bring their children to Jesus, a place where their children can be touched and blessed by Him.

One of the fastest ways to get Guaranteed Growth is through having an excellent children's ministry where children can experience God in a real way. I believe in the old saying; it takes a village to raise a child.

> **ONE OF THE FASTEST WAYS TO GET GUARANTEED GROWTH IS THROUGH HAVING AN EXCELLENT CHILDREN'S MINISTRY WHERE CHILDREN CAN EXPERIENCE GOD IN A REAL WAY.**

MY STORY

This has been my experience with my five girls. My wife and I have done the best we can to pass our faith to our children, but if it wasn't for our dynamic children's and youth ministry reinforcing the faith lessons we were passing on to them at home, they would have never become the wonderful young ladies they are today. It was in our children's ministry that my girls memorized a big part of the scriptures they know today. It was in our children's ministry that they volunteered for the first time and learned to serve. It was in our youth ministry where they found out and developed their ministry gifts and are using them today. I thank God every day for our children's and youth ministry. My wife and I know that we couldn't have done it without them.

When a family is making a decision on what church they will attend, their children are going to be a major part in the decision process. After every service, every parent asks their children, "How did you enjoy class? What did you learn?" Their answer will determine the chances of that family returning.

Businesses that are catering to whole families understand how important it is to market and include children in their vision. They know if they capture the hearts and attention of the children, they get the parents in the process. That's why McDonald's, Chick Fil-A and Chuck E. Cheese have playgrounds, happy meals, and cartoon characters to attract the kids to their places of business. I recently came across an article that stated that no company in the world distributes more toys than McDonald's. McDonald's knows that if the kids love McDonald's, they will make sure their parents take them there.

Every parent wants to make their children happy and successful. A church that has an excellent children's ministry can help parents accomplish these two goals.

The admonition Jesus gave the disciples was, "Let the children come to me. Don't stop them!" A church that doesn't minister to the children can be doing the same thing the disciples were doing, stopping the children from coming to Jesus. The disciples were not kid-friendly. Let's not be like them, but like Jesus. Jesus not only loves the children, but He says the kingdom of heaven is theirs. Children are not just a group on the list, they are God's top priority. Jesus said that children are the greatest in the Kingdom. Jesus always welcomed the children and so should we.

CHILDREN ARE NOT JUST A GROUP ON THE LIST, THEY ARE GOD'S TOP PRIORITY.

Luke 9:47-48 (NLT)
"But Jesus knew their thoughts,
so he brought a little child to
his side. 48 Then he said to them, 'Anyone who
welcomes a little child like this on
my behalf welcomes me, and anyone who
welcomes me also welcomes my Father
who sent me. Whoever is the least among you
is the greatest.'"

Jesus gives us an amazing promise that anyone who welcomes a little child on His behalf welcomes Him.

Jesus is making a very important point that if we make welcoming children our goal, we will also be welcoming Jesus into our churches. This means that a church that loves children will be attractive to the parents and attractive to Jesus. Let's create an atmosphere where the children, parents and Jesus are welcomed. A vibrant children's ministry is a win-win proposition that will always result in Guaranteed Growth.

REASON #3 - CHILDREN ARE GREAT EVANGELISTS!

Children have great faith and are also great evangelists. They will come and bring their friends and family. Every week we hear a testimony of a parent that has come to the church for the first time and they say that the reason they came is because their children kept inviting them. We have many children that have come to church on their own through our buses, walked to church or were brought by their friends. We teach these children to pray for the salvation of their family. When children are taught that they need to evangelize, they are tenacious. They will not give up until they see the person they are praying for come to church.

OUR STORY

One of the greatest examples I've seen of this principle is an outreach we did at the local baseball stadium.

God gave us the vision and strategy on how to fill the stadium. Reach the children and the children will fill the stadium. God opened doors for us to be able to do assemblies at the local schools. After every assembly, we invited the children and told them that if they came with their parents, we would have a brand-new bike for them at our outreach event. People started donating bikes and children signed up to get tickets for the event. On the day of the outreach, not only did the children come, but they brought their friends and family. Over five thousand people came and filled that stadium and about 2,000 people got saved that day. The whole infield of that baseball stadium was full of people giving their lives to Jesus. What an amazing day! It was all made possible by the children. They did the job of filling that stadium. A ministry that focuses on children will see Guaranteed Growth, because the children can't help themselves, they will evangelize. Children will always share their experiences with great passion and influence with their loved ones. Even Jesus, when He was a child, brought His parents to church.

Luke 2:45-46 (NKJV)
"So when they did not find Him, they returned to Jerusalem, seeking Him. 46. Now so it was that after three days they found Him in the temple, sitting in the midst of the teachers, both listening to them and asking them questions."

The fact will always be that where the children are, the parents will follow. "Reverse evangelism" works. Let's not underestimate the children. They will bring Guaranteed Growth.

REASON #4 - OUR CHILDREN WILL BE OUR FUTURE LEADERS!

We have a responsibility to pass on our faith to our children. If we teach them the Word of God, we will see a harvest of future leaders and volunteers that will come out of the ranks of our children's ministry. We can't afford to be short sighted and not see God's destiny for our children. They will not be kids forever. Every child has a great kingdom assignment in them. It's our job to train them and point them in the way they should go, so that when they are older, they will be a blessing to their families, communities and local church. This must be intentional and will take a lot of work on our part. Our responsibility is not only to our immediate family, but also to all the children of the world. We must do all we can to bring them to our churches and disciple them to become future world changers in their own right. The future of the church is dependent on how many leaders and volunteers we can develop to replace our present leadership and volunteer base. If we don't replace ourselves, the church as we know it, will not exist and be virtually extinct. We can't let that happen. Our children are our future leaders and volunteers. Any ministry that focuses on developing children will not only experience present growth, but future growth as well. The next generation should do more than we ever did. Let's believe in them and prepare them for their purpose.

> **ANY MINISTRY THAT FOCUSES ON DEVELOPING CHILDREN WILL NOT ONLY EXPERIENCE PRESENT GROWTH, BUT FUTURE GROWTH AS WELL.**

CHAPTER TEN

HOW TO BUILD PRINCIPLE #5
TEN PRACTICAL STEPS TO BUILD A SUCCESSFUL CHILDREN'S MINISTRY

CHAPTER 10

HOW TO BUILD PRINCIPLE #5

TEN PRACTICAL STEPS TO BUILD A SUCCESSFUL CHILDREN'S MINISTRY

Psalms 78:4-6 (NLT)
"We will not hide these truths from our children; we will tell
the next generation about the glorious deeds of the Lord, about his power and his
mighty wonders. 5 For he issued his laws to Jacob; he gave his instructions to
Israel. He commanded our ancestors to teach them to their children, 6 so the next
generation might know them— even the children not yet born— and they in turn
will teach their own children."

OUR STORY

From the first day we opened the church, I knew that our children's ministry was going to be important in our church. As a pastor, I prayed for a children's pastor that was called to minister to children with passion and a high level of creativity. God answered my prayer, just like He would answer any one of our prayers. God sent me the greatest children's Pastor in the world, Suzie Zavala. Every year, we are reaching out to thousands of inner-city kids with God's love. Today, she is a world class leader, but it didn't start out that way. I asked her to write her story of how she became the leader we see today. She is a prime example of how important children's ministry is and how our future leaders will be trained through our children's ministries.

This is Susie's story, a testimony that will reveal how important a children's ministry is in developing future leaders...

SUSIE'S STORY

> *I am 'Miss Susie.' I am blessed and honored to be a Children's Pastor and I am a living testimony of how the love of Jesus, through children's ministry, can change a child's life forever. I grew up in a gang-infested, poverty-stricken neighborhood. Within the walls of my own home, I faced alcoholic parents, rejection, physical and verbal abuse from my very own dad. However, God had better plans for me then to get caught up in the drug game or gangs I grew up in. He protected me and sent people who were not my parents to show me His love, while my parents couldn't. Their names were Mr. and Mrs.*

Hicks, and they changed my life forever. Mr. and Mrs. Hicks were on assignment to reach me with the love of God, to fight for me, to believe in me and to plant the seeds in me, that one day would become 'Kid's World' (our children's ministry). They did not look at the house or family I came from, they didn't look at my clothes, they didn't pay attention to the outward appearances of my life, but they looked deeper and saw value in me that I could not even see in myself. They saw a hurting little girl who needed love and they loved me unconditionally; they loved me with the heart of Jesus.

Every week, I would look forward to hearing that loud horn of the church bus coming down the street to pick me up. I was so excited to get to our local church, where I was loved and accepted. It was a place that was fun and full of joy and excitement, it was a place where I knew I was safe, a place that would bless me for the rest of my life, and a place where my purpose was planted through the hope and prayers of these two selfless, committed people of God.

Today, I am a mother and grandmother and I have been married for more than twenty-five years to an amazing man. I am able to serve the Lord and reach his children. I did not become a statistic, or a product of my environment, because I said yes to Jesus.

Looking at my world, I can see just how different my life would have been if I never would have been introduced to Jesus. I have a twin brother, who does not know Jesus yet. We share the same birthday, and we grew up in the same household, but he has been in and out of state prison most of his adult life. That is where the lifestyle of our upbringing usually leads, and that is exactly what the love of Jesus saved me from. Mr. and Mrs. Hicks passed away when I was only ten years old. It's been thirty-plus years since they left this world, but their legacy is still alive in my heart today. It was because they took me on, as their personal ministry assignment, that I was able to lead both my parents to Jesus and I was able to forgive my parents for their mistakes. It is because of them that I was able to experience what God's love looks like, and it is because of them that I am able to minister to thousands of hurting children every day. Kid's World is not only their seed, it is their legacy. This legacy only continues to grow as we continue to raise up the leaders for tomorrow.

Kid's World reaches out to the inner-city's children through weekly services, a bus ministry, relationships, and personal support. We believe that with the unique opportunity to reach children, we are able to reach entire families as well. We give hope to the hopeless, teach children about Jesus, and raise them up in the ways of the Lord to become responsible, God fearing, active church members who lead others to Christ as well. We take our mission of 'reaching the world one kid at a time' very seriously, and focus on personally connecting with each child individually and meeting their own personal and specific needs. Our kids grow up and are 'on fire' for God. Many of them have taken the excitement of Kid's World into their adult lives and ministries. They have been discipled well and their lives have been forever changed in the walls and playgrounds of Kid's World.

A successful children's ministry is vital to a thriving church. God has given us a recipe to create a successful children's ministry that impacts the lives of children so deeply.

> **A SUCCESSFUL CHILDREN'S MINISTRY IS VITAL TO A THRIVING CHURCH.**

10 PRACTICAL STEPS TO BUILD A SUCCESSFUL CHILDREN'S MINISTRY!

1. Visit a church that is already doing a successful children's ministry and take good notes. If they can do it, you can too.
2. Get a vision of what you want your children's ministry to look like and write it down.
3. Passionately share vision and pray for workers.
4. Constantly recruit workers.
5. As soon as you can, hire a children's pastor.
6. Get a curriculum that you will use and train, train, and train.
7. Make children's ministry the most fun and exciting place on earth. (We are competing with Disneyland).
8. Be willing to invest a major part of finances to children's ministry. (Classrooms, curriculum, transportation, props, technology, games, etc.)
9. Do children's outreaches. (They will come and hear the Word. You can get a crowd of children anywhere. Use this as an opportunity to invite them and sign them up for church and the next big event.)
10. Most of all - create an atmosphere of God's love. Nothing will grow without love!

Now that we realize the necessity of a healthy children's ministry, we need a lot of volunteers to serve our children. The next principle we will cover for Guaranteed Growth is how to build a strong volunteer team.

CHAPTER 10

ACTION PLAN

FOR CREATING AN EXCELLENT CHILDREN'S MINISTRY

LIST 5 THINGS YOU CAN APPLY FROM THIS CHAPTER
TO EXPERIENCE GUARANTEED GROWTH

#1

#2

#3

#4

#5

CHAPTER ELEVEN

PRINCIPLE #6 — "A CHURCH THAT FINDS A PLACE FOR EVERYONE TO SERVE IS GUARANTEED TO GROW!"

CHAPTER 11

PRINCIPLE #6 – A CHURCH THAT FINDS A PLACE FOR EVERYONE TO SERVE IS GUARANTEED TO GROW!

There is one common denominator in churches that are growing and it is a large group of people that are serving. In order to experience "Guaranteed Growth" we must develop a culture where everyone realizes their responsibility to serve in the local church. We should have an expectation from every member in the church, to come to our worship services ready to receive what God has for them and also a readiness to serve. We have a saying in our church that promotes the culture we are looking to develop, "Receive in one service and serve in another." Since we have fourteen worship services each week and over 100 active ministries, no one has an excuse for not serving. The more people we have actively serving, the stronger our church becomes. We must always keep track of this area of ministry. If the number of people serving is not growing, our church is not growing. This will always be one of the most challenging areas of ministry, because we need to constantly be recruiting, training, plugging people in, and expanding our ministries.

> **IF THE NUMBER OF PEOPLE SERVING IS NOT GROWING, OUR CHURCH IS NOT GROWING.**

THE TWO AREAS OF GREATEST SPIRITUAL WARFARE ARE SALVATION AND SERVING

#1 - SALVATION! THE ENEMY WILL DO ALL HE CAN TO PREVENT PEOPLE FROM BELIEVING IN JESUS AND BEING SAVED!

Luke 8:12 (NKJV)
"Those by the wayside are the ones who hear; then the devil comes and takes away the word out of their hearts, lest they should believe and be saved."

There is a real devil that is constantly strategizing to hinder people from hearing the Gospel and being saved. As a church, we have been commissioned to preach the Gospel to all nations. When people hear the Gospel, they have an opportunity to believe and be saved. Since we know that the only way souls are going to be saved is by preaching the Gospel, we must continue to tell people about Jesus. We can't forget it's all about souls being saved, not just gathering a crowd. I made a promise to God that I would never have a service without presenting the Gospel and as a result we have never had a service where someone has not gotten saved. The Gospel works. The enemy knows that he can't stop everyone from being saved, so his next strategy is to do all he can to stop people from serving and fulfilling their God-given purpose.

#2 - SERVING! THE ENEMY WILL DO ALL HE CAN TO STOP PEOPLE FROM SERVING!

If the devil has not succeeded in stopping us from being saved, he will do all he can to hinder us from connecting to the local body of Christ through serving. When Jesus called His disciples, He called them not only to follow Him, but He also called them to serve. After a person gets saved, the next step is discipleship training with the purpose of getting the believer equipped to serve and disciple others. The assignment of every leader in the church is to equip the people to do the work of the ministry.

> **AFTER A PERSON GETS SAVED, THE NEXT STEP IS DISCIPLESHIP TRAINING WITH THE PURPOSE OF GETTING THE BELIEVER EQUIPPED TO SERVE AND DISCIPLE OTHERS.**

Ephesians 4:11-12 (NKJV)
"And He himself gave some to be apostles, some prophets, some evangelists, and some pastors and teachers, 12 for the equipping of the saints for the work of ministry, for the edifying of the body of Christ."

After someone gets saved, they must graduate to serving in the local church. If this is not happening, people will eventually get bored and leave the church. It's like a football team only practicing and never having a game. There would be no purpose for all the training. The church must be careful that they are not taking this same approach—a whole bunch of preaching and teaching and not enough doing.

WHAT ARE THE BENEFITS OF FINDING A PLACE FOR EVERYONE TO SERVE?

These benefits will lead to Guaranteed Growth.

BENEFIT #1 - WHEN PEOPLE SERVE, THEY BECOME COMMITTED TO THE VISION OF THE CHURCH!

When people are serving, they are investing. The two areas that we treasure the most, is our time and money.

There is a spiritual principle we can't ignore "where our treasure is, that's where our heart will be also."

> *Luke 12:34 (NKJV)*
> *"For where your treasure is,*
> *there your heart will be also."*

If we can get people to invest their time and resources, we will have their hearts. A person that doesn't give and serve will be unstable and uncommitted. That's the last thing we need, a congregation full of people that are superficially committed and, as a result become critical and non-supportive. Getting people to serve is a must if the local church is going to be healthy and be able to fulfill the vision of God.

> **GETTING PEOPLE TO SERVE IS A MUST IF THE LOCAL CHURCH IS GOING TO BE HEALTHY AND BE ABLE TO FULFILL THE VISION OF GOD.**

BENEFIT #2 - A CHURCH THAT SERVES IS SPIRITUALY HEALTHY!

A church with a large servant base is healthy, because the people are growing and fulfilling their purpose. Until people are serving, they are not functioning according to design. Every person is a masterpiece created for good works. We are created to serve!

Ephesians 2:10 (NLT)
"For we are God's masterpiece. He has created us anew in Christ Jesus, so we can do the good things he planned for us long ago."

A believer that is not using his gifts to serve is not doing what they were created to do and therefore will begin to feel a deep dissatisfaction. A person that is not serving is not functioning according to design. We call this being dysfunctional. In every area that we are experiencing dysfunction, there will be breakdowns. Many of our breakdowns in our marriages, relationships and churches are a direct result of self-centeredness.

Serving others is a way of defeating a self-centered mindset. We can never have a healthy church or relationships with a bunch of self-centered people that only want to be served and are not willing to give back to their church and community. A church that does not have a culture of everyone serving each other, will eventually self-destruct. I believe the cause of many church splits is a direct result of people having too much time on their hands, because they are just standing around and not actively getting involved in ministry. The members become full of discontent, gossip, and instability.

> **A CHURCH THAT DOES NOT HAVE A CULTURE OF EVERYONE SERVING EACH OTHER, WILL EVENTUALLY SELF-DESTRUCT.**

If a church is not involved in finding needs and meeting them through the participation of the body of Christ, it is asking for trouble. I would never endorse church splits, but I believe some of them are necessary because some churches have not created a place for everyone to serve. People are desperate to see God use them and fulfill their purpose. They know there is more. It takes a lot of work to find a place for everyone to serve, but in the long run it will be worth it, especially when we see all the ministry that is being done and the growth that is being created. A healthy church is a church where the people are unified, and everyone is doing their part. There is nothing like walking into an atmosphere where the majority of the people are serving, there is electricity in the air, the people come in expecting for God to move and are full of joy. Doing the Father's will is spiritual nourishment and, therefore, it produces spiritual health. A church that is not serving is spiritually malnourished and will eventually die. Jesus explained a spiritual principle - that spiritual nourishment comes from doing the will of God.

John 4:34 (NLT)
"Then Jesus explained: 'My nourishment comes from doing the will of God, who sent me, and from finishing his work.'"

In this scripture Jesus was ministering to the lady at the well, while His disciples where busy eating. A church that is busy just eating and receiving, but never serving will be unhealthy in the long run and lose its spiritual perspective. There is nourishment that can only be attained through serving others. This nourishment will result in joy, peace, personal fulfillment, and Guaranteed Growth in the church. Nothing grows without feeding it. God has made serving Him and others a major source of strength and nourishment.

A healthy church will always experience Guaranteed Growth, because healthy sheep reproduce. We see this in this scripture, the lady at the well receives spiritual nourishment from Jesus and immediately goes out and serves her community by sharing with others what she received from Jesus. This is a healthy exchange. She receives and then she gives, as a result many became believers, a whole city was reached. That city experienced "Guaranteed Growth," because one lady whose name isn't even mentioned is served and then serves. This lady at the well served her community at the highest level by bringing them to Jesus. Our acts of service done in the spirit of love will always cause the kingdom of heaven to expand. People see Jesus in the hearts of His servants.

> **A HEALTHY CHURCH WILL ALWAYS EXPERIENCE GUARANTEED GROWTH, BECAUSE HEALTHY SHEEP REPRODUCE.**

John 4:39(NLT)
"Many Samaritans from the village believed in Jesus because the woman had said, 'He told me everything I ever did!'"

If we want to see many come to Jesus, we need to create a community of believers that aren't just hearing, but also doing. We must always remember the Words of Jesus that, "Spiritual nourishment or health comes from doing the Father's will."

BENEFIT #3 - WHEN PEOPLE ARE SERVING, THEY USUALLY BRING OTHERS WITH THEM.

The more involved people get, the more excited they are about what God is doing in their local church. When people are excited, they share that excitement and it will always lead to inviting their friends and relatives to join them. Billy Graham knew this principle well. He knew how many people would attend his crusades, based on how many people he had committed to serving. No one usually comes alone. For every person serving we can multiply that number by three and that would give a good estimate of the attendance of that event. We have seen these numbers prove themselves over and over. If we can get one hundred people committed to serve, we will have at least three hundred in attendance. Our best advertisement is through the members of our own church. Every week, I meet people that have come to the church for the first time and I always ask them who invited them and the majority of the time they will say a friend or relative that already attends and is serving.

> **FOR EVERY PERSON SERVING WE CAN MULTIPLY THAT NUMBER BY THREE AND THAT WOULD GIVE A GOOD ESTIMATE OF THE ATTENDANCE OF THAT EVENT.**

BENEFIT #4 - WE WILL BE ABLE TO SERVE MORE PEOPLE!

(The bigger the net/organization the more people we can serve.)

Our churches have a capacity, a saturation point. We can only serve the amount of people we are prepared to serve. We can't serve 5,000 people with two workers. It's impossible. If our servant base does not expand, our capacity doesn't either. God will not give us more than we are prepared to handle. I remember that there was a ministry team that visited our church and they brought a hundred altar workers. My initial thought was, "They have too many people working the altar for the amount of people that will come forward to receive prayer". To my surprise, when the altar call was made there was just over one-hundred people who came forward that Sunday Night service, to receive Jesus as their Lord and savior. Was it a coincidence? I don't think so. I believe that God knew they were ready to serve over a hundred souls, so he sent them. God will not send us souls that we are not prepared to serve. I learned a big lesson that day, that we as a church were putting a lid on what God could do, because we didn't have enough people serving.

A great example of the principle of capacity is the childless woman. God gave this woman a Word that she would be blessed with many children. He told her to enlarge her house and spare no expense, because He was ready to fill it. The only limit was the level that she expanded. God could not fill a room she had not built. It's the same principle. God will not bring growth in a ministry that is not prepared to receive it.

Isaiah 54:1-3(NLT)
"'Sing, O childless woman, you who have never given birth! Break into loud and joyful song, O Jerusalem, you who have never been in labor. For the desolate woman now has more children than the woman who lives with her husband,' says the Lord.
2 'Enlarge your house; build an addition. Spread out your home, and spare no expense!
3 For you will soon be bursting at the seams. Your descendants will occupy other nations and resettle the ruined cities.'"

The more servants we have in place the bigger our net is. A fisherman knows that the size of his net will determine the amount of fish he can catch. If our volunteer net does not grow, neither will our results. It's time for us to think and prepare bigger than we have, so we can receive bigger than we have received.

> **THE MORE SERVANTS WE HAVE IN PLACE THE BIGGER OUR NET IS.**

BENEFIT #5 - WE WILL BE ABLE TO EXPAND AND DEVELOP NEW MINISTRIES

We should never get to the point that we are not birthing out new ministries. Healthy churches are always reaching out to new groups of people that are in need. Every time we find a new need, we find a new area of potential growth.

When Nehemiah realized that the people were suffering because the walls were destroyed, he took ownership of the assignment of rebuilding the walls of Jerusalem. It would have been easy, just like everyone else in Jerusalem, to acknowledge and ignore the need. We never want to get to the place where we become blind to the pain, hurt and poverty around us. As Nehemiah took ownership of the people in

Jerusalem, God would bring all the resources and help he needed to fulfill the vision. This is exactly how a ministry is built. It starts with a man or woman recognizing a need, taking ownership and then building a team to minister to that need. Wherever there is a need, there is an opportunity to expand our ministry base. The more active ministries we have in our church, the more people that will have a place to serve and the more people we can reach with the love of God.

When we are expanding, we rarely will have all the people we need to do the expansion. It never fails. New people will come out of the wood work to fill all the new spots that were created. We can create a demand for more servants by taking ownership of needs that we discover and being willing to build the teams to meet those needs.

> **WE CAN CREATE A DEMAND FOR MORE SERVANTS BY TAKING OWNERSHIP OF NEEDS THAT WE DISCOVER AND BEING WILLING TO BUILD THE TEAMS TO MEET THOSE NEEDS.**

New ministries cause growth in a few areas:

Growth Area #1 - God will send laborers.

Growth Area #2 - We will now be able to minister to a new group of people.
Growth Area #3 - New leaders will be developed.

BENEFIT #6 - WE WILL BE FORCED TO DEVELOP MORE LEADERS TO HANDLE THE GROWTH.

The more leaders we have in place, the more people we can disciple to maturity and place into ministry. Leaders will come from three areas, assistant leaders that are presently serving in the ministry, people in the congregation that have been there the whole time, and leaders that God will send to fortify the ministry. Usually all the leaders we will need are already in our congregation and have not been discovered. Pastor Tommy Barnett said, "The miracle is in the house." The First place we should look is in our house. We can only grow at the level of our leadership base. The demand that is being created by all the ministry expansion and, all the people that are signing up to get involved, will force us to develop leaders. Our present leadership can't do it all. Moses was faced with the same dilemma and had to delegate his responsibilities to others.

Exodus 18:18-21(NLT)
"You're going to wear yourself out—and the people, too. This job is too heavy a burden for you to handle all by yourself. 19 Now listen to me, and let me give

you a word of advice, and may God be with you. You should continue to be the people's representative before God, bringing their disputes to him. 20 Teach them God's decrees, and give them his instructions. Show them how to conduct their lives. 21 But select from all the people some capable, honest men who fear God and hate bribes. Appoint them as leaders over groups of one thousand, one hundred, fifty, and ten.

The original apostles ran into the same problem. The church grew so fast that they had to assign leaders to distribute the food so that they could continue praying, studying and expanding the church.

Acts 6:2-4 (NLT)
So the Twelve called a meeting of all the believers. They said, "We apostles should spend our time teaching the word of God, not running a food program. 3 And so, brothers, select seven men who are well respected and are full of the Spirit and wisdom. We will give them this responsibility. 4 Then we apostles can spend our time in prayer and teaching the word."

BENEFIT #7 - WE WILL HAVE GREATER FINANCIAL SUPPORT

This is an obvious point, the more people that are serving the more people that are giving. The most generous and consistent givers are those that are involved through serving. They see themselves as part of the team that is building the dream. There will always be a strong correlation between generosity and a servant's heart. It's one in the same. Everyone who begins to serve will move to another level of worship and intimacy with God. When someone is willing to give their time and talents to serve, they have moved into the core of the church, moving towards the inner circle. They now look at the church as their home, and as a result, feel a deepened sense of responsibility to take care of it in every way. Let's do all we can to get as many people as we can into the inner circle of the church through serving. If our inner circle is growing, so is every other area of ministry including finances. These finances are a must, if we are going to be able to continually expand the church, ministries and staff needed to support the ministry.

EVERYONE WHO BEGINS TO SERVE WILL MOVE TO ANOTHER LEVEL OF WORSHIP AND INTIMACY WITH GOD.

CHAPTER TWELVE
HOW TO BUILD PRINCIPLE #6
EIGHT PRACTICAL STEPS TO BUILDING A STRONG SERVANT BASE

CHAPTER 12

HOW TO BUILD PRINCIPLE #6

EIGHT PRACTICAL STEPS TO BUILDING A STRONG SERVANT BASE

STEP #1 - START A SERIES ON THE IMPORTANCE OF SERVING!

We did a series and named it, "I Am a Servant." We designed a t-shirt, which I wore every Sunday during the series. We also urged everyone to get a t-shirt and wear it on a big day we called "I Am a Servant Day." On this day, we had the congregation come out and serve the church and the community. Not only was this an exciting day of serving, but it was also one of our biggest days of recruiting new servants to our present ministries. By the time the series was done, the congregation gained a new identity—"I Am a Servant." We don't just serve...we are servants—it's who we are. This changed the culture of our church. The congregation was so proud to be part of a church that serves their community.

STEP #2 - PLAN AN OUTREACH THAT YOU NEED A LOT OF VOLUNTEERS AND ANNOUNCE IT FOR AT LEAST A MONTH

Have sign ups every week, make flyers, put it in the weekly bulletin, make an exciting video announcement. This outreach will be a rallying point for your ministry. This will be another turning point of the culture of the church. As a leader of the ministry, you must plan two to three major outreaches a year to keep the church focused on serving and recruiting. During these outreaches, new people and talent will be discovered. The outreaches are worth it, even if all you did was to get the church serving, but obviously, that won't be the only benefit.

> **YOU MUST PLAN TWO TO THREE MAJOR OUTREACHES A YEAR TO KEEP THE CHURCH FOCUSED ON SERVING AND RECRUITING.**

All the community that was served will also be blessed and will cause many of them to make a choice to come to your church and join the "Servant Revolution."

STEP #3 - ASSIGN A LEADER THAT IS IN CHARGE OF GETTING PEOPLE INVOLVED AND CONNECTED TO MINISTRY TEAMS

This person is so important that eventually, they should be a full-time staff member. In our church, the title for this position is ministry development director. Their role is simple, develop a great relationship with all present ministry team leaders, and constantly help people get connected to their purpose in serving. The person we have is a right-hand person in the ministry and we couldn't do it without her. Her name is Janet Casas. She is totally passionate about her role of helping build teams and helping people find their place in the body of Christ. She has also built a team called, "The Get Connected Team," the team that is building the dream. They have weekly connection meetings, where everyone that wants to get involved in serving gets an introduction to all the ministries they can serve in. After this meeting, servants sign up for at least one ministry and the team introduces them to ministry leaders. A lot of follow up must be done to get new people assimilated into teams, but it will be worth it when you see the people happily fulfilling their purpose. Remember - a person that serves is a happy person.

STEP #4 - SIT DOWN WITH EACH MINISTRY TEAM LEADER AND SET GOALS OF HOW MANY PEOPLE THEY ENVISION GETTING INVOLVED

During the meeting, you set a goal of how many people you want to see serving, but you also identify where that person will serve in the ministry. We have created an organizational chart that the leader is to fill out to keep track of ministry development. The chart has all the positions that need to be filled. For example, it has a place for the name of the leader of the ministry, it asks for name of assistant leader and slots for all the names of all the servants that are presently serving along with open spots for all the people needed for the ministry to operate at the optimum. The organizational chart not only puts the vision on paper, but it also holds that leader accountable. As a leader you can look at that chart and see if a ministry is growing or stagnant.

(Email a request to Resources@GuaranteedGrowth.Life to receive an Example of an Organizational Chart)

STEP #5 - MAKE A "GET CONNECTED" CARD THAT CAN BE FILLED OUT ON THE WEBSITE, APP OR IN PERSON

On this "Get Connected" card, put all the major ministries with a box next to each ministry. Each box can be checked off when choosing a ministry, and should include a place where volunteers can put their contact information. If serving is going to be part of the culture, both the electronic and hard copy of this card must be everywhere and in every part of the discipleship process. We have "Get Connected" cards in front of every seat and located in multiple places on our website and app. Our website should not just be informational but it should be a place where people can connect to their place of service in the ministry.

The "Get Connected" card is introduced in every service, in our membership class and in every one of our discipleship classes. We never stop recruiting. It's the life blood of the church. Until our members go from being saved to serving, they are not planted and therefore will never bear fruit and the fruit is other souls being saved. I know it takes time to create these systems, but in the long run it will enable our churches to grow but still be easy to connect with at the same time. The easier it is to connect the faster our churches can grow. Let's make sure we are creating easy ways for our people to connect.

> **WE NEVER STOP RECRUITING. IT'S THE LIFE BLOOD OF THE CHURCH.**

STEP #6 - HAVE EVERY TEAM MAKE A TRAINING MANUAL

It's important to have consistent training. The only way to have consistent training is to get it on paper. In order to duplicate effective servants, we need to get all protocols and expectations on paper. If it's not on paper, it will not be duplicatable. Unless we get all of our training in paper manuals, we have not built a ministry that can be passed on to others. If we have a really good leader that has all of the training in his head and has not transferred it into a manual, the church has put itself in a vulnerable position. If that leader decides to leave, we will have to start all over and lose all the momentum that we have built up to that point. The great thing about having well written training manuals is that anyone can use them for training and develop effective servants.

STEP #7 - EXPAND TO ANOTHER SERVICE

The rule of thumb to determine whether we need to expand to another worship service is eighty percent capacity. If the room is filled at 80%, it's time to expand to another service.

OUR STORY

We started our church with one 10:30am Sunday service, then we expanded to two services after the 10:30am service was filled to 80%. When expanded, we also changed our service times to a 9:00am and 11:00am service. We proceeded to add 1:00pm service, 3:30pm service, 6:00pm service and a mid-week service on Wednesday night, which happens to be our biggest service of the week. We continue to expand every time we get to eighty percent capacity. At the time of writing, we are now at a combined total of 14 weekly worship services at our Main and Downtown campus. With every expansion, we are able to get more people involved, create new teams, develop new leaders, and attract a whole new group of people. Every new service becomes a whole new congregation. It takes a lot of work to continue to expand. But, I've come to realize, if we are not expanding...we are dying. Expand or die. Every successful organization understands this principle.

STEP #8 - START A NEW MINISTRY

Every time we discover a new need, we have potentially discovered a new ministry. We always want to serve our church and community with greater effectiveness and excellence. We discovered that there was a sector of the population of our community and church that was being neglected and it was "Special Needs" children. So, we launched a new ministry that serves our special needs children and their families. With this new ministry, we have new leaders, assistant leaders, servants, and families that are now part of our church. If it wasn't for this new ministry, we would have missed out on a big opportunity to be a blessing to these families in need of support. Every time the Holy Spirit reveals a group of people that are hurting and in desperate need of God's help, we do our best to create a ministry that will meet that need and as a result experience "Guaranteed Growth".

> **WE DO OUR BEST TO CREATE A MINISTRY THAT WILL MEET THAT NEED AND AS A RESULT EXPERIENCE "GUARANTEED GROWTH".**

I am excited to see how this chapter will cause a refocus or new approach to getting people involved. Every person is just waiting to be asked to make a difference. Everyone desires to feel wanted and longs to fulfill their God given purpose. A growing ministry is always a result of reaching new people, helping them discover their purpose and placing them in a position where they can do it. Remember- "Any church that finds a place for people to serve is guaranteed to grow."

CHAPTER 12

ACTION PLAN

FOR CREATING A PLACE FOR EVERYONE TO SERVE

LIST 5 THINGS YOU CAN APPLY FROM THIS CHAPTER
TO EXPERIENCE GUARANTEED GROWTH

#1
#2
#3
#4
#5

CHAPTER THIRTEEN

PRINCIPLE #7 — "A CHURCH THAT PREACHES THE GOSPEL AND MAKES A CALL TO RESPOND IS GUARANTEED TO GROW!"

CHAPTER 13

PRINCIPLE #7 – A CHURCH THAT PREACHES THE GOSPEL AND MAKES A CALL TO RESPOND IS GUARANTEED TO GROW!

I call this "casting the net." The Holy Spirit will send the fish where the nets are being thrown. Jesus said, "come follow me and I will make you fishers of men." When we first started our church, I made a commitment to God that we would never have a worship service without making an altar call. What I meant by an altar call, is giving everyone present an opportunity to be born again by responding to a public call to declare their choice to repent of their sins and confess Jesus as their personal Lord and savior. We are moving towards our sixteenth year of ministry and we have never had a service that we have not seen at least one person come to Christ and experience the greatest miracle of all—salvation! I believe what God's word says that if we lift Jesus up, He will draw all men to himself.

John 12:32 (NLT)
"And when I am lifted up from the earth,
I will draw everyone to myself."

Every time we come together, we should lift up the name of Jesus by presenting a clear declaration of the Gospel. The power of God to save is in the proclamation of the Gospel. We need to declare that we are not ashamed of the gospel of Jesus Christ. Without the proclamation of the Gospel, our churches and ministries will not see souls being saved and as a result be spiritually dead. A church that is dead is not growing. The best way to see revival in a ministry is to get back to the great commission - preaching the Gospel of Christ!

> **A CHURCH THAT IS DEAD IS NOT GROWING. THE BEST WAY TO SEE REVIVAL IN A MINISTRY IS TO GET BACK TO THE GREAT COMMISSION - PREACHING THE GOSPEL OF CHRIST!**

Romans 1:16 (NKJV)
"For I am not ashamed of the gospel of Christ, for it is the power of God to salvation for everyone who believes, for the Jew first and also for the Greek."

Wherever the good news of Jesus is presented souls will be saved! If souls are being saved, the church is guaranteed to grow! After the Gospel is presented, it's time to ask all present to respond to the call to follow

Jesus. Jesus did it. He asked every one of His disciples to follow Him and they did.

THE KINGDOM OF HEAVEN ONLY EXPANDS WHEN A SOUL IS SAVED BY PUTTING THEIR FAITH IN JESUS.

Matthew 4:19 (NKJV)
"Then He said to them, 'Follow Me,
and I will make you fishers of men.'"

The truth is not everyone that is called will follow. It is also true that no one will follow that hasn't been called or asked. Church growth is not our main goal, kingdom growth is. Not all church growth is kingdom growth. The kingdom of heaven only expands when a soul is saved by putting their faith in Jesus. We can grow our churches with just church transfer, but if that's the only growth we are experiencing, we are fooling ourselves into thinking that we are expanding the kingdom. A church that is not seeing the lost come to Jesus on a regular basis is not fulfilling its ultimate purpose of making disciples of all men.

Matthew 28:19 (NLT)
"Therefore, go and make disciples of all the nations,
baptizing them in the name of the Father and the
Son and the Holy Spirit."

CHAPTER FOURTEEN

HOW TO BUILD PRINCIPLE #7
FIVE STEPS TO MAKE A SUCCESSFUL CALL TO SALVATION

CHAPTER 14

HOW TO BUILD PRINCIPLE #7

FIVE STEPS TO MAKE A SUCCESSFUL CALL TO SALVATION HOW DO WE MAKE AN ALTAR CALL?

STEP #1 - PROCLAIM THE GOOD NEWS OF JESUS CHRIST!

Let them know what Jesus has done for them. He absolutely loves them and has provided a way for everyone to receive the free gift of eternal life through faith in Jesus Christ. Salvation is not a reward for good behavior. It is an act of undeserved kindness. Jesus paid the penalty for every one of our sins. No one needs to continue living under the guilt and shame of the past. Everyone can be saved and set free! Let them know that they can bring their pain, hurt, addictions, and sins to Jesus and He will forgive and give them the free gift of eternal life. We need to be careful that the church doesn't become a self-help seminar that just teaches great principles for success and never presents the Gospel. We can help people to succeed and be great motivators, but if we never present the Gospel, the Holy Spirit will never have the opportunity to move in their hearts and bring them to a place of repentance of their sins and salvation through faith in Jesus Christ.

Mark 16:15-16 (NLT)
"And then he told them, 'Go into all the world and preach the Good News to everyone. 16. Anyone who believes and is baptized will be saved. But anyone who refuses to believe will be condemned.'"

We need to get some old fashion preaching of the Good News back in our churches. Jesus has given all believers the assignment to preach the Good News. There is nothing more powerful than the Gospel of Jesus Christ. After the preaching of the Gospel, comes signs and wonders and salvation of lost souls. No other message in the world can save a soul for eternity. The miracle of the regeneration of a soul only happens one way. The Gospel of Jesus Christ is preached and then people believe and are saved. The pattern is always the same. The Gospel is preached, then people believe, and miracles happen.

Mark 16:17 NLT
"These miraculous signs will accompany those who believe: They will cast out demons in my name, and they will speak in new languages."

If we want to see the glory of God back in our churches, we need to begin with a recommitment to the preaching of the Gospel. The preaching of the Gospel is not psychology, principles of success or positive speaking, but pointing people to the sacrifice that Christ has made for their sins. It's not that we won't teach on all these subjects, but let's make sure we always bring it back to the Gospel.

> **LET'S MAKE SURE WE ALWAYS BRING IT BACK TO THE GOSPEL.**

STEP #2 - ASK THEM POINT BLANK—"IF YOU WERE TO DIE TODAY WHERE WOULD YOU SPEND ETERNITY?"

We need to bring people to a point of decision. Some might say to themselves. "I think I will go to heaven, because I am a good person or... I think I will go to heaven, because I belong to a certain church or went through a series of classes." At this point, we need to emphasize that we are not saved by our good works, but solely by putting our faith in the finished work of Jesus Christ.

Romans 3:22-24 (NLT)
"We are made right with God by placing our faith in Jesus Christ. And this is true for everyone who believes, no matter who we are. 23 For everyone has sinned; we all fall short of God's glorious standard. 24 Yet God freely and graciously declares that we are righteous. He did this through Christ Jesus when he freed us from the penalty for our sins."

Heaven is not for perfect people. It will be full of sinners that have been saved by grace! One of the greatest enemies to salvation is self-righteousness and religion. Instead of people putting their trust in Jesus to save them, they have put their trust in themselves or a religious institution.

Our main goal is not to change behavior or get people to join our church. Our main goal is to get people saved and introduce them to an amazing relationship with Jesus Christ. After presenting the Gospel and addressing some of the misconceptions that they might have, the Holy Spirit will do what we can't do. It is the Holy Spirit that opens spiritual eyes, convicts of sins and gives the free gift of eternal life.

John 16:8 (NLT)
"And when he comes, he will convict the world of its sin, and of God's righteousness, and of the coming judgment."

The truth is without putting their faith in Jesus Christ, they will end up in a real hell for eternity. If we have not preached the Gospel, their blood will be on our shoulders. We must not be intimated by the politically-correct church that will not mention hell. Jesus is our example. He talked more about hell than anyone else in scripture.

> **WE MUST NOT BE INTIMATED BY THE POLITICALLY-CORRECT CHURCH THAT WILL NOT MENTION HELL.**

Luke 12:4-5 (NLT)
"Dear friends, don't be afraid of those who want to kill your body; they cannot do any more to you after that. 5 But I'll tell you whom to fear. Fear God, who has the power to kill you and then throw you into hell. Yes, He's the one to fear."

When they realize that their sin has a future penalty and that Jesus is the only one that can save them, they can now make a clear choice to accept or reject the love of Christ. All who believe and accept Jesus are born again and become children of God, which is the biggest miracle of all!

John 1:11-13 (NLT)
"He came to his own people, and even they rejected him. 12 But to all who believed him and accepted him, he gave the right to become children of God. 13 They are reborn not with a physical birth resulting from human passion or plan, but a birth that comes from God."

STEP #3 - MAKE THE CALL!

Give them an opportunity to publicly declare their choice to believe and confess Jesus as their Lord and savior. We need to determine what works best for us. I usually make a bold call by having them raise their hands after I count to three. The number three has no great significance but it prepares their hearts to respond. The majority of the time I don't have them bow their heads and close their eyes because if they are ashamed to make a public declaration to follow Christ in the church, they will never follow Him outside the church. I will always emphasize that if they acknowledge Him before men, Jesus will acknowledge them before the Father.

Following Jesus is a choice that we can't be ashamed of. We need to let go of all pride and humble ourselves by willingly confessing Him publicly as our Lord and Savior.

Matthew 10:32-33 (NLT)
"Everyone who acknowledges me publicly here on earth, I will also acknowledge before my Father in heaven. 33 But everyone who denies me here on earth, I will also deny before my Father in heaven."

Jesus died publicly for all of us, now it's time for us to help the people to publicly make a stand to follow Christ!

STEP #4 – HAVE THEM TAKE ACTION!

After they have raised their hands, it's time to take the next action step, ask them to come forward or stand in their place. This is their first step to following Christ. This is a symbol of them leaving their old lives in those seats and starting a new walk with Christ. As they take that step of faith, we begin to see the move of the Spirit of God upon their lives. Many will begin to cry and be set free as soon as they begin to walk forward or stand. They are now exercising their faith and allowing the Holy Spirit to touch them for the first time in their lives. This moment becomes their own personal encounter with their loving, Heavenly Father. The God they only heard about, they are experiencing for themselves. Even the disciples had to take a step to follow Jesus. They followed him with steps of action. The bolder we get the greater move of God we will see in our ministries and in people's lives. God has not given us a spirit of fear and timidity. We will never see a great revival or growth, without bold and consistent altar calls. The call to take action, after they raised their hands is solidifying their decision to follow Christ.

2 Timothy 1:7 (NLT)
"For God has not given us a spirit of fear and timidity, but of power, love, and self-discipline."

Let's make bold altar calls and expect bold responses!

STEP #5 - GET THEIR INFORMATION AND PRAY FOR THEM!

The altar team should be trained to love them and welcome them to the family of God. They should be trained to get their information. This is the first step of discipleship for the new believer. This is a perfect time to minister to them in prayer. After we've had them fill out an altar card and pray with them, we should sign them up for their next step in spiritual growth with a handout that clearly maps out their growth journey.

In our church, we've made it very easy, we have a saying, "It's as easy as 1, 2, 3!" We've simplified our discipleship process into 3 easy steps. Their first step is our foundational classes called Starting @ The Way, their second step is Prospering @ The Way, with the final third step being Freedom @ The Way. Every church needs to create a clear path for the people to walk through that best works for them. Everything starts with giving the opportunity for someone to respond to the message of the Good News of Jesus Christ! Making bold altar calls, will always lead to Guaranteed Growth. The Holy Spirit will always send people to a church that is preaching the Gospel and calling people to be disciples of Jesus Christ! Now that they're saved and have begun the process of discipleship, we will discuss a principle in the next chapter on how we care for the people.

CHAPTER 14

ACTION PLAN

FOR CREATING SUCCESFUL CALLS TO SALVATION

LIST 5 THINGS YOU CAN APPLY FROM THIS CHAPTER TO EXPERIENCE GUARANTEED GROWTH

#1

#2

#3

#4

#5

CHAPTER FIFTEEN

PRINCIPLE #8 — "A CHURCH THAT CARES FOR PEOPLE THROUGH VIBRANT SMALL GROUPS IS GUARANTEED TO GROW!"

CHAPTER 15

PRINCIPLE #8 – A CHURCH THAT CARES FOR PEOPLE THROUGH VIBRANT SMALL GROUPS IS GUARANTEED TO GROW!

WHAT IS A SMALL GROUP?

A small group is a group of two to twelve people that meet on a regular basis (example: daily, weekly or monthly). The purpose of the group is to study the Bible, to love and take care of one another, build relationships, disciple others, develop leaders, and do life and ministry together. The group can meet at church, in a home, in a break room, at work or any other designated area. Every small group has a leader that has been recruited and trained to lead the group. A small group should also have an assistant leader and host that has opened their home or provides a place to meet. The assistant leader is there to help the small group leader disciple and take care of the people, while personally being trained and developed to lead their own small group.

MY INITIAL RESISTANCE TO SMALL GROUPS

I, as a Pastor, struggled with the idea of small groups, because I thought it was just another church fad. I eventually changed my mind when our church ran into a growth barrier that we seemingly couldn't break through. During this time, there was no growth, no matter how hard we worked. Week after week, the church attendance stayed the same and at times it felt like our church was in a decline. I desperately needed to discover whatever was hindering our church from growing so that we would regain our spiritual health and continue to grow. I guess I had to learn this lesson the hard way. After years of doing ministry, I discovered a major mistake that I had made. My error was not developing a system to build leaders that would take care of and disciple the people. It became very obvious to me why the church wasn't growing. People were leaving as fast as they were coming, because we couldn't take care of them and disciple them. The complaints and back door of the church got bigger and bigger.

A church without small groups can become difficult for the congregants to connect with and as a result make them feel lonely. I began to understand why the fastest growing churches in the world all had vibrant small group ministries. Without small groups, the needs of the people in the church would, unintentionally, be neglected and the people would experience minimal spiritual growth. I found out that no matter how spiritual and talented the pastors or leaders were, they would not be able to meet all the needs of a growing congregation without trained people in place to disciple and take care of them. I learned that every time our church had a growth spurt, we reached a place of saturation or maximum capacity. What I mean by maximum capacity is that our present leaders were taking care and discipling as many people as they could with their limited abilities and time constraints. Without building new leaders and small groups, the church will not be able to continue to grow. We have been at this place of maximum capacity many times during our last 16 years and that's why we have made leadership and small group development one of our main goals.

> **WITHOUT SMALL GROUPS, THE NEEDS OF THE PEOPLE IN THE CHURCH WOULD, UNINTENTIONALLY, BE NEGLECTED AND THE PEOPLE WOULD EXPERIENCE MINIMAL SPIRITUAL GROWTH.**

Remember, it's our responsibility as the leaders of the church to intentionally equip the body of Christ to lovingly serve and care for one another. Small groups and leadership development will never happen accidentally, it must become a system that is integrated into our church infrastructure and culture.

Ephesians 4:12 (ERV)
"Christ gave these gifts to prepare God's holy people for the work of serving, to make the body of Christ stronger."

Serving: (diakonia/dē-ä-ko-nē'-ä) service to others, ministering, those who help meet the needs of others, the service of those who prepare and present food, waiter, an attendant.

MY STORY ON SMALL GROUPS (CONTINUED)

Small groups were no longer just an option, they were now a necessity. Without small groups, we would become just another hard-working church with good intentions, that was not growing. As I began to open up to the idea of small groups, the Holy Spirit took me back to my own spiritual roots. He brought to my memory how smalls groups were there at the very beginning of my walk with God. I'm so thankful that the Holy Spirit brought back to remembrance what I needed to know to overcome and breakthrough the growth barriers we were facing as a church. I pray that the Holy Spirit will birth in you the same desire and revelation that he put in my heart to take care of the people and disciple them through the development of small groups.

My first experience with small groups started in my own home. My mother always had a small group bible study. I didn't know that our little bible study is what we call today a small group or life group. I also didn't know how important it was in the big picture of a healthy growing church. I will never forget those weekly bible studies. I am who I am today because of the deposits made in me in those intimate small group meetings.

It was in this small group setting where my mom passed on her faith to me. So many great things came out of those bible studies, I grew to know Jesus as my personal Lord and Savior, many of my friends were introduced to Jesus Christ, I met my wife and learned how to disciple others for Christ. It has now been over thirty years since I attended those home bible study meetings, but I can still remember the lessons I learned and the impact it made on my character and spiritual development. If it wasn't for those home bible studies, I wouldn't have had the spiritual foundation I have today. A foundation that has enabled me to be the leader I needed to be for my family and church. I am forever indebted to my mother's commitment to invest in me through those weekly small group meetings. That small group bible study not only changed my life, but it has multiplied into thousands of people coming to know Jesus as Lord and Savior. If it wasn't for this small group bible study, I would have never learned the skills that I needed to plant a church.

I have learned to never underestimate the power of small beginnings. Everything great starts out small. Without a small seed, we will never see a big harvest.

> **NEVER UNDERESTIMATE THE POWER OF SMALL BEGINNINGS. EVERYTHING GREAT STARTS OUT SMALL. WITHOUT A SMALL SEED, WE WILL NEVER SEE A BIG HARVEST.**

Zechariah 4:10 (EXB)
"The people should not think that small beginnings are unimportant [For who despises the day of small things?]"

Later in life, I also had a small group that I held at my house. I led that small group for over fifteen years. My mother experienced the greatest fruit that anyone can ever have, and that is duplication. She duplicated herself in me by teaching me the word of God and by teaching me how to lead a small group myself. I was now doing what my mother taught me to do. The small group that I started has multiplied into hundreds of small groups in our church that are impacting thousands of lives. My mom would have never known that her small group would have turned into a mega church that's doing world-wide ministry. Jesus taught us this principle. He knew that His small group of twelve would do greater things than even He did. You never know who God is training through you in a small group that will go and change the world.

> **YOU NEVER KNOW WHO GOD IS TRAINING THROUGH YOU IN A SMALL GROUP THAT WILL GO AND CHANGE THE WORLD.**

John 14:12 (NLT)
"I tell you the truth, anyone who believes in me will do the same works I have done, and even greater works, because I am going to be with the Father."

The goal still remains the same, duplication that leads to multiplication. My expectation is that the ones I am presently discipling in my small group, will eventually lead small groups themselves and also train others to do so. Jesus had the same expectations with His disciples. The goal was never for His disciples to stay with him forever in His circle but that they would go out and create discipleship circles of their own.

Many of those people in my original small group have ended up being some of the most effective leaders in our church today and are also leading small groups and ministries themselves. Until we become effective in developing and leading small groups, we will never be entrusted or be able to lead great organizations.

Matthew 25:23 (AMP)
"His master said to him, 'Well done, good and faithful servant. You have been faithful and trustworthy over a little, I will put you in charge of many things; share in the joy of your master.'"

The fact is that without developing our small group ministry to take care of the people, our ability to grow will be hindered forever. Thank God that there is an answer. All we have to do is make an intentional effort to focus on building small groups that will take care and disciple the people that God has entrusted us with.

Now that I have done my best to introduce you to small groups, let's discover how small groups played a major part in Jesus' ministry and the early development of the church.

WHY SHOULD YOUR CHURCH HAVE SMALL GROUPS?

1. JESUS HAD A SMALL GROUP

Jesus did not start with a crowd of thousands. Jesus started His ministry by recruiting a small group of twelve disciples. His style of developing others is still the most effective way to bring people into a mature relationship with God. Jesus often spoke to big crowds but, at the end of the day, He would retreat to His original twelve and pour into them. A great example of Jesus meeting with His disciples privately, after a public teaching, was when He taught the parable of the farmer planting seeds. Following his public teaching, Jesus had a private session where His disciples who would ask Him further questions in reference to the teaching. Jesus would give them privileged insight that the crowd never got.

> **JESUS STARTED HIS MINISTRY BY RECRUITING A SMALL GROUP OF TWELVE DISCIPLES.**

Luke 8:9-11 (NLT)
"His disciples asked him what this parable meant.
10 He replied, 'You are permitted to understand the

secrets of the Kingdom of God. But I use parables to teach the others so that the Scriptures might be fulfilled: "When they look, they won't really see. When they hear, they won't understand."
11 This is the meaning of the parable: The seed is God's word.'"

The original disciples had the same experience I had with my mother. They started their spiritual education in a small group of twelve, with Jesus being the leader. What an amazing small group that must have been. Imagine Jesus being your small group leader. I have good news. Jesus has given us a promise, that every time we meet in a small group, He will be there with us as well.

Matthew 18:20 (NKJV)
"For where two or three are gathered together in My name,
I am there in the midst of them."

Jesus could have easily said any time a crowd comes together I will be there, but He started with the least common denominator, the number two. We should not underestimate a small group meeting. God still does big things in small groups. Jesus is reminding us that every time we get together, in a small group of two or more, in His name, He will show up and teach and touch us the same way He did with His original disciples. There are certain encounters that we are going to have with Jesus that will only happen in a small group setting. We can lead people to Christ through the big crowds, but we can only disciple them in small groups. Let's follow Jesus' lead!

Jesus showed us how to disciple people and build a growing ministry. We build growing churches by building people through one on one meetings and small group settings.

Until we get good at the small, we will never be able to sustain the big. The main goal isn't growth. Our goal should be to love, take care and disciple the people that God has given us responsibility over.

Once we learn how to properly disciple one, we can eventually minister and disciple many. Let's go back to the basics and begin discipling and taking of care of people the way Jesus did, in groups of no more than twelve.

ADVISE: Some quick advice to new pastors - Don't wait for the big crowds to come in because of your great teaching or worship team. Start building a thriving ministry by developing small group leaders that will help you take care of the people as they come in. Now, let's move on to the second reason that we need small groups. Small groups were embedded in the foundation of the early church.

2. THE EARLY CHURCH HAD SMALL GROUPS

Jesus didn't change the pattern of discipleship, even after He resurrected from the dead. Let's look at some examples of small groups in the early church.

***FIRST EXAMPLE OF SMALL GROUPS IN THE EARLY CHURCH:** JESUS MEETS WITH HIS DISCIPLES IN A SMALL GROUP AFTER HE RESURRECTS FROM THE DEAD.*

Before Jesus went to the cross, He set an appointment with His disciples to meet Him at a familiar mountain in Galilee. This mountain must have been one of the regular places that Jesus met with His disciples in their small group sessions. What stands out about this particular meeting is the timing of it. It was to be held after His death and resurrection. Just think about it, Jesus is ready to suffer and die for the sins of the world and He is setting an appointment with His remaining eleven disciples for their next small group meeting. The scripture below shows us two things about Christ. The first thing is that small groups were important to Jesus, and secondly, that the pattern for discipleship is still the same, even after Jesus died and resurrected.

Matthew 28:16-18 (NLT)
"Then the eleven disciples left for Galilee, going to the mountain where Jesus had told them to go. 17 When they saw him, they worshiped him— but some of them doubted! 18 Jesus came and told his disciples, 'I have been given all authority in heaven and on earth.'"

Small groups were not just a pre-resurrection thing. They are a kingdom thing that will be here as long as the church exists on earth.

SECOND EXAMPLE: *JESUS TELLS THE DISCIPLES TO MEET IN A SMALL GROUP TO RECEIVE THE BAPTISM OF THE HOLY SPIRIT*

In one of those small group sessions that Jesus had with His disciples after His resurrection, He gave them instructions to meet in a small group for their next God encounter.

Acts 1:3-5 (NLT)
"During the forty days after he suffered and died, he appeared to the apostles from time to time, and he proved to them in many ways that he was actually alive. And he talked to them about the Kingdom of God. 4 Once when he was eating with them, he commanded them, 'Do not leave Jerusalem until the Father sends you the gift he promised, as I told you

before. 5 John baptized with water, but in just a few days you will be baptized with the Holy Spirit.'"

This small group meeting was not held in a church, but in an upper room of a house. In this meeting they would be empowered by the Holy Spirit to be witnesses of Jesus throughout the world. God still uses small group meetings to equip and empower His people do to great exploits for Him.

> **GOD STILL USES SMALL GROUP MEETINGS TO EQUIP AND EMPOWER HIS PEOPLE DO TO GREAT EXPLOITS FOR HIM.**

Acts 2:2-4 (NLT)
"Suddenly, there was a sound from heaven like the roaring of a mighty windstorm, and it filled the house where they were sitting. 3 Then, what looked like flames or tongues of fire appeared and settled on each of them.
4 And everyone present was filled with the Holy Spirit and began speaking in other languages, as the Holy Spirit gave them this ability."

THIRD EXAMPLE: *THE EARLY CHURCH NOT ONLY MET IN PUBLIC PLACES, BUT THEY ALSO MET DAILY IN SMALL HOME GROUPS*

After Jesus ascended to the Father, His disciples continued His pattern of making disciples. They taught the early church to continue to meet together in the church, but also in homes or small group settings.

Acts 5:42 (NLT)
"And every day, in the Temple and from house to house, they continued to teach and preach this message: 'Jesus is the Messiah.'"

The early church met together in larger groups, at the temple or in synagogues for corporate worship, but also in small groups, in the homes of believers. Small groups especially played a crucial role in the early church when persecution hit. Persecution drove the church underground. The early church needed small groups for its survival. During intense times of persecution, the church is not able to meet openly. It can only survive through small groups. Any church that has a healthy small group ministry becomes persecution proof. We need to build churches that are structured in such a way that the enemy, government, and new laws can't hinder its progress. There are places all over the world where Christianity is illegal, and the only way they can meet is in small groups that are held in secret places. Small groups will never be obsolete and will always make the church resilient.

SMALL GROUPS WILL NEVER BE OBSOLETE AND WILL ALWAYS MAKE THE CHURCH RESILIENT.

FOURTH EXAMPLE: *SMALL GROUPS WERE USED AS A PLACE OF PRAYER IN THE EARLY CHURCH*

After Peter was miraculously released from prison, he knew where to go. He went to the home of Mary. He went to a small group that he knew met daily to study and pray.

Acts 12:11-12 (NLT)
"Peter finally came to his senses. 'It's really true!' he said. 'The Lord has sent his angel and saved me from Herod and from what the Jewish leaders had planned to do to me!' 12 When he realized this, he went to the home of Mary, the mother of John Mark, where many were gathered for prayer."

FIFTH EXAMPLE: *SMALL GROUPS WERE CONSIDERED HOUSE CHURCHES*

Small groups, or house churches, were used as a foundation or a building block of establishing churches in new cities.

Romans 16:5 (NLT)
"Also give my greetings to the church that meets in their home. Greet my dear friend Epenetus. He was the first person from the province of Asia to become a follower of Christ."

I believe a great way to plant a new church in any region or city, is by first establishing a healthy small group in that area. The best assignment we can give a new pastor is to first build a healthy small group and learn how to take care of those people with the love of God. All the lessons that are needed to lead a healthy growing church can be learned in a small group setting. The truth is if a pastor can't build a small group and learn to multiply that group, he is not ready or able to build a growing church.

ALL THE LESSONS THAT ARE NEEDED TO LEAD A HEALTHY GROWING CHURCH CAN BE LEARNED IN A SMALL GROUP SETTING.

CHAPTER SIXTEEN
HOW TO BUILD PRINCIPLE #8
EIGHT GOALS FOR CREATING VIBRANT SMALL GROUPS

CHAPTER 16

HOW TO BUILD PRINCIPLE #8

EIGHT GOALS OF A SMALL GROUP THAT LEAD TO GUARANTEED GROWTH

GOAL #1- LOVE AND TAKE CARE OF THE PEOPLE

Taking care of people is what ministry is all about. The church exists to carry out this initiative that was given to us by Jesus himself. Jesus totally emphasized the value of loving people and caring for them in the majority of His ministry teachings. A great example of Jesus' focus on caring for His people was the conversation He had with Peter right after He resurrected from the dead. We should pay careful attention to all of Jesus' teachings, but I think we should pay special attention to everything He said after He rose from the dead. Every one of these conversations are meant to be a summary or a conclusion of everything Jesus ever taught while He was alive on earth. In this conversation, Jesus focuses on the most important question that He could ever ask a believer. Do you love me? Jesus goes on to tell Peter and every believer how to love Him. We love Him by feeding and taking care of His sheep or people.

John 21:15-17 (NLT)
"After breakfast Jesus asked Simon Peter,
'Simon son of John, do you love me more than these?'
'Yes, Lord,' Peter replied, 'you know I love you.'
'Then feed my lambs,' Jesus told him.
16 Jesus repeated the question:
'Simon son of John, do you love me?' 'Yes, Lord,' Peter said, 'you know I love you.'
'Then take care of my sheep,' Jesus said. 17 A third time he asked him,
'Simon son of John, do you love me?'
Peter was hurt that Jesus asked the question
a third time.
He said, 'Lord, you know everything.
You know that I love you.'
Jesus said, 'Then feed my sheep.'"

In these two verses, Jesus reminds Peter of the two greatest commands in the Bible: to love God and love your neighbor as you love yourself.

Matthew 22:36-39 (NLT)
"'Teacher, which is the most important commandment in the law of Moses?' 37 Jesus replied, 'You must love the Lord your God with all your heart, all your soul,

and all your mind.' 38 This is the first and greatest commandment. 39 A second is equally important: 'Love your neighbor as yourself.'"

We can't say we love God and not love and take care of the people he has put under our care. Jesus takes the subject of taking care of others very serious and personal and so should we. He is clearly saying that if we don't feed and take care of one another, we are not expressing our love for Him.

> **JESUS TAKES THE SUBJECT OF TAKING CARE OF OTHERS VERY SERIOUS AND PERSONAL AND SO SHOULD WE.**

Matthew 25:40 (ERV)
"Then the king will answer, 'The truth is, anything you did for any of my people here, you also did for me.'"

We feed and take care of the lambs by teaching them the Word of God and by lovingly meeting their needs. Small groups are a great place for this to happen. There is not a pastor in the world that is able to personally take care of all the needs of the local church. This assignment to feed and care must be evenly distributed to all believers and trained small group leaders.

*Feed: (boskō) - promote in every way the spiritual welfare of the members of the church.

*Care: (poimainō) - to look after; watch over and care for, minister to, or wait on with service, to nourish, to cherish, and serve as you would your own body, to supply what the soul needs, to shepherd.

A church that properly feeds and cares for the lambs or people through its ministries and small groups will always produce healthy sheep, that will in turn, reproduce healthy lambs. Remember, shepherds don't produce lambs, healthy sheep do. In order for the sheep to become healthy enough to be fruitful, they must be fed well and taken care of. When the sheep are healthy, they will cause the church to grow by reproducing themselves. Even though the assignment that Jesus has given us is clear, it still seems to be a major challenge for most churches and believers.

> **A CHURCH THAT PROPERLY FEEDS AND CARES FOR THE LAMBS OR PEOPLE THROUGH ITS MINISTRIES AND SMALL GROUPS WILL ALWAYS PRODUCE HEALTHY SHEEP, THAT WILL IN TURN, REPRODUCE HEALTHY LAMBS.**

Every growing church will eventually get to a place where taking care and loving the people will become difficult. When the church is small, the pastor and few leaders can meet the needs of the congregation. But as it grows, a gap will naturally occur between the amount of people that are coming and the amount of leaders and small groups needed to properly take care of them. This gap is one of the major reasons why churches stop growing. The early church ran into the same problem. The church grew so fast that it outgrew its leadership and servant base. It got to the point where the people started complaining that they were not being taken care of.

Acts 6:1-7 (NLT)
"But as the believers rapidly multiplied, there were rumblings of discontent. The Greek-speaking believers complained about the Hebrew-speaking believers, saying that their widows were being discriminated against in the daily distribution of food."

The apostles knew that if they didn't call and develop new leaders to take care of the church that it couldn't continue to grow. Only after seven new leaders were selected and put in place did the church continue to spiritually grow and increase in numbers.

Acts 6:2-7 (NLT)
"So the Twelve called a meeting of all the believers. They said, 'We apostles should spend our time teaching the word of God, not running a food program. 3 And so, brothers, select seven men who are well respected and are full

of the Spirit and wisdom. We will give them this responsibility. 4 Then we apostles can spend our time in prayer and teaching the word.' 5 Everyone liked this idea, and they chose the following: Stephen (a man full of faith and the Holy Spirit), Philip, Procorus, Nicanor, Timon, Parmenas, and Nicolas of Antioch (an earlier convert to the Jewish faith).6 These seven were presented to the apostles, who prayed for them as they laid their hands on them. 7 So God's message continued to spread. The number of believers greatly increased in Jerusalem, and many of the Jewish priests were converted, too."

An inability to develop small groups and leaders to take care of the people will not only hinder the church from being effective and growing, but it will also cause the church to eventually lose its most productive people.

Our most productive people are those that seem to fit in anywhere and do the majority of the ministry in the church. These great people will eventually get to a place of maximum saturation, where they can't personally take care of more people, and begin to feel overwhelmed. Just like we need to take care of the masses we also need to take care and support our hard working leaders in our churches. If they are not alleviated from the burden, they can get to a place of burn-out and quit, or worse-case scenario leave the church. Building small groups is one of the most caring things we can do not only because it gives us the ability to love and take of more people but it is also a way to care of our present leaders by alleviating some of their burden.

GOAL #2 - MAKE DISCIPLES OF JESUS CHRIST THROUGH THE TEACHING OF GOD'S WORD AND TRAINING

Matthew 28:20 (NLT)
"Teach these new disciples to obey all the commands I have given you. And be sure of this: I am with you always, even to the end of the age."

Jesus did not commission us to make believers, but to make disciples. The making of a disciple is not an easy or natural process. In order to make a disciple we must first become a disciple of Jesus Christ ourselves. We become a disciple by submitting ourselves to being mentored by a more experienced believer. Secondly, we must personally accept the call to become a disciple maker. Thirdly, as a disciple maker we need to go out of our way and find people to disciple, this is called recruiting. Fourthly, once we have recruited some people to be discipled, we need to spend time with them on a regular and consistent basis. The time that we spend with them can be broken down into two categories; one on one time and group time. True discipleship only happens through the building of deep relationships and this is accomplished through intentional fellowship. It is through these regularly scheduled meetings that we pass on our faith, build relationships and train them to be disciples of Jesus Christ that make disciples of Jesus Christ.

> **IN ORDER TO MAKE A DISCIPLE WE MUST FIRST BECOME A DISCIPLE OF JESUS CHRIST OURSELVES.**

GOAL #3- DEVELOP LIFE LONG RELATIONSHIPS

Relationships are the most important ingredient to church growth. If we did a survey of how the majority of our members came to our church, ninety-nine percent of them would tell you that they came through a friend or family member. The reason that they came is the same reason that they will stay, and that's relationships. There are no short cuts to building healthy relationships. The only way to build healthy relationships is by spending quality time with the people we are discipling. Small groups provide a structure and schedule to build lifelong relationships.

> **SMALL GROUPS PROVIDE A STRUCTURE AND SCHEDULE TO BUILD LIFELONG RELATIONSHIPS.**

Small groups are an easy place to develop intimate relationships. During these meetings, we get to know one another more intimately and begin to discover each other's personal needs. There is no greater way to show the love of God, than being there for someone in their time of crisis. Small groups provide an opportunity for us to show the love of God when people need us most. No one should ever feel that they are going through it alone. Small groups provide an inner circle of friends that are there to share our pain and concerns with. Without this inner circle of friends we can easily go back to our old acquaintances for help and be tempted to regress to the old lifestyle that God has delivered us from. It is a shame anytime that the world is more accessible and caring than the local church. Small groups that intentionally go out of their way to build relationships and make sure that the people are being taking care of are the best glue to keep the people coming.

It is a fact that people come and stay in our churches because of the loving relationships they have built. When people are connected to healthy relationships, the church becomes irresistible and they will find it hard to leave even in difficult times. In order to build these tight-knit relationships, we spend intimate and quality time with people and one of the most productive ways for us to accomplish that is through our small group meetings.

Some churches can't grow to the next level, because they are "platform churches". What I mean by a platform church is that the people are coming just because they like what they see on the stage. In other words, they love the way the pastor preaches or the way the worship team sings. Don't get me wrong, I believe that every church should have a platform that is attractive, but a church that stays as a platform church will always be vulnerable to huge attendance swings based on what is happening on the platform. We need to go the next level and move the church from a platform church to a relational church.

When the church becomes a relational church, people will begin to say that what they love the most about the church is the relationships they have built. Relationships are a far better way to build a strong church rather than just depending on the performances that we see on the stage.

> **RELATIONSHIPS ARE A FAR BETTER WAY TO BUILD A STRONG CHURCH RATHER THAN JUST DEPENDING ON THE PERFORMANCES THAT WE SEE ON THE STAGE.**

The only way to move from a platform church to a relational church is by making small groups and relationship building a top priority. Small groups provide a place for these two priorities to happen. In small groups our members will be able to meet and interact with people they would have never met. Relationship miracles happen in small groups.

MY STORY

A great example of a relationship miracle that happened for me in a small group, is the meeting of my wife. What a great bonus to my small group meeting. She was invited by one of her friends to this small group and the first night she attended she gave her life to Jesus. I am not saying start a small group and get a wife or husband, but I am saying God has some wonderful people he wants you to meet and some of those people are going to play a very important role in your life. Thank God for small groups that make sure no one ends up feeling like an outsider and gives a place for everyone to belong.

GOAL #4 - DEVELOP LEADERS - SMALL GROUPS ARE A LEADERSHIP DEVELOPMENT FACTORY

The greatest use of our time is developing people. Jesus spent His three years of ministry personally training His disciples to be fishers of men, in others words, men of influence. It wouldn't have mattered how many miracles Jesus did, if He never trained and encouraged His disciples to be leaders that would develop people and change the world.

Jesus had two main goals while He was on earth. The first goal was to seek and save the lost, and the second was to train the found to be like Him. When we develop another leader to be like Jesus, we have now accomplished one of the greatest assignments we can carry out on earth. A church that doesn't develop new leaders to care, teach and disciple others will never experience exponential growth. A church cannot grow beyond their leadership base. Every time we develop a new leader, we have just expanded our spiritual net and will have the capacity to care and disciple a larger group of people.

It is through small groups that we pass on our faith and the teachings of Christ to the next generation of believers. It is also through small groups that we train and develop new leaders to take care of the people. In the scripture below, we see the pattern for personal discipleship and leadership development that the Apostle Paul passed on to Timothy.

2 Timothy 2:2 (NLT)
"You have heard me teach things that have been confirmed by many reliable witnesses. Now teach these truths to other trustworthy people who will be able to pass them on to others."

The pattern for discipleship and church growth is still the same. We learn from the teachings of our spiritual mentors and we pass on what we've learned, to trustworthy people, who will in turn, pass them on to others. Paul got this pattern from Jesus himself. Everything Jesus did was an example of how we should do ministry. Jesus would not only take care and protect His disciples, He would also make it His mission to train them to become effective leaders themselves. I pray that the Holy Spirit will convince you of this spiritual truth. The truth is that the most effective way to disciple and develop leaders is still through intimate small group settings just like Jesus had.

GOAL #5 - INVITE NEW PEOPLE TO JOIN - SMALL GROUPS ARE A GREAT PLACE TO INVITE OUR FRIENDS AND FAMILY TO BE INTRODUCED TO CHRIST AND THE CHURCH

Every time that a small group grows because someone is recruited, the church grows. If a church has twenty-five small groups, and each small group just reaches two people a month, the church will grow by fifty people a month, and in a year the church will grow by six-hundred people. Most people would be more inclined to accept an invitation to a home bible study than a church service. The resistance to Christ and the church can be broken down in a loving home setting or a breakroom bible study, especially when surrounded by familiar faces. We must remember that true evangelism is a person to person process of sharing the Good News and intimate conversations. Small groups are a natural place for both of these elements to happen. When our small groups are loving and inclusive, people will be drawn to them, led to Christ, and bridged to the local church. Our small groups can be one of our biggest doors for people to know Christ and join the local church. Let's keep all our doors open.

> **WHEN OUR SMALL GROUPS ARE LOVING AND INCLUSIVE, PEOPLE WILL BE DRAWN TO THEM, LED TO CHRIST, AND BRIDGED TO THE LOCAL CHURCH.**

If a church has twenty-five small groups, it also has twenty-five open doors for people to come into the Kingdom of God and our church. When small groups become evangelical, the church will grow by leaps and bounds with new disciples of Jesus Christ and be able to take care of many more people. If someone comes to the salvation knowledge of Christ through a small group, the care and discipleship of that individual is organic. He or she has started out their walk with God in a place where they will be discipled and naturally be taken care of. The bottom line is that healthy small groups attract and keep new members. So why wouldn't we build them for the glory of God?

WARNING: One of the inherent weaknesses of any small group is the natural tendency to become exclusive instead of inclusive. Every group must be reminded on a weekly basis, that they are called to tell others about the Good News of Jesus Christ. Every small group must do the work of telling others about Christ.

2 Timothy 4:5 (NLT)
"But you should keep a clear mind in every situation. Don't be afraid of suffering for the Lord. Work at telling others the Good News, and fully carry out the ministry God has given you."

GOAL #6 - GIVE AN OPPORTUNITY FOR THE PEOPLE TO OPEN UP AND SHARE

Miracles happen when people open up and share their struggles, insight, and gifts. A small group leader is a facilitator more than a preacher or teacher. What I mean by being a facilitator is that his job is to lead the people to open up by asking them questions. An effective small group leader doesn't give all the answers. He gives an opportunity for The Holy Spirit to speak to them. The members of the group should learn how to hear and trust the voice of The Holy Spirit. The greatest miracle anyone can have is learning to discern the voice of God in their lives. As the people begin to open up, it is important that we don't make them feel dumb. The win happens when they open up their mouths and start to participate. Remember if someone doesn't feel comfortable enough to speak, they will never be comfortable enough to open up with their secret life, share their pain, struggles of the past, or sins that they are presently dealing with. When someone finally opens up and begins to speak, they are now ready for a miracle. Not only do we want them confident enough to talk within the group, we also want them confident enough to use their spiritual gifts to minister to one another. Everything is working according to plan when everyone is participating and sharing their gifts with everyone in attendance.

> **WHEN SOMEONE FINALLY OPENS UP AND BEGINS TO SPEAK, THEY ARE NOW READY FOR A MIRACLE.**

Jesus was really good at getting people to open up and participate in their own miracles. Jesus was the perfect small group facilitator. A great example of Jesus facilitating a conversation and leading someone to the biggest miracle of all, salvation, is the Samaritan woman at the well. How did Jesus do it? He did it by asking her questions that caused her to open up and receive the greatest gift of all, faith in Christ as one's own personal Lord and Savior.

John 4:7-26 (NLT)

When a Samaritan woman came to draw water, Jesus said to her, "Will you give me a drink?" 8 (His disciples had gone into the town to buy food.) 9 The Samaritan woman said to him, "You are a Jew and I am a Samaritan woman. How can you ask me for a drink?" (For Jews do not associate with Samaritans.) 10 Jesus answered her, "If you knew the gift of God and who it is that asks you for a drink, you would have asked him and he would have given you living water." 11 "Sir," the woman said, "you have nothing to draw with and the well is deep. Where can you get this living water? 12 Are you greater than our father Jacob, who gave us the well and drank from it himself, as did also his sons and his livestock?"

13 Jesus answered, "Everyone who drinks this water will be thirsty again, 14 but whoever drinks the water I give them will never thirst. Indeed, the water I give them will become in them a spring of water welling up to eternal life."

15 The woman said to him, "Sir, give me this water so that I won't get thirsty and have to keep coming here to draw water." 16 He told her,

"Go, call your husband and come back."

17 "I have no husband," she replied.

Jesus said to her, "You are right when you say you have no husband. 18 The fact is, you have had five husbands, and the man you now have is not your husband. What you have just said is quite true." 19 "Sir," the woman said, "I can see that you are a prophet. 20 Our ancestors worshiped on this mountain, but you Jews claim that the place where we must worship is in Jerusalem." 21 "Woman," Jesus replied, "believe me, a time is coming when you will worship the Father neither on this mountain nor in Jerusalem. 22 You Samaritans worship what you do not know; we worship what we do know, for salvation is from the Jews. 23 Yet a time is coming and has now come when the true worshipers will worship the Father in the Spirit and in truth, for they are the kind of worshipers the Father seeks. 24 God is spirit, and his worshipers must worship in the Spirit and in truth."

25 The woman said, "I know that Messiah" (called Christ) "is coming. When he comes, he will explain everything to us."

26 Then Jesus declared, "I, the one speaking to you—I am he."

Here in this scripture we see Jesus effectively leading the Samaritan to open up and share. A healthy small group meeting should look a lot more like a conversation than a lecture and that's why our small groups shouldn't be larger than twelve. The bigger the group the less people share and the less spiritual transformation that happens.

> A HEALTHY SMALL GROUP MEETING SHOULD LOOK A LOT MORE LIKE A CONVERSATION THAN A LECTURE AND THAT'S WHY OUR SMALL GROUPS SHOULDN'T BE LARGER THAN TWELVE.

GOAL #7 - CARRY OUT THE VISION OF THE LOCAL CHURCH

Every small group should look at themselves as a ministry team that is ready to be deployed at any time in order to fulfill the vision that God has for the local church body. Small groups shouldn't just minister to those in their small group family, but they should also minister to the church family, as a whole. An effective small group always has a big picture mentality. It was never meant to be independent or disconnected from the church body. A healthy, small group sees themselves as an extension or branch of the local church body that is there to reach the community, disciple believers, and carry out the vision of the church. When the church is doing a major city outreach, fund raising campaign, or launching a new set of discipleship classes, each small group leader should be informed and be on board, so that they can use all of their delegated influence to move everyone in the group towards the fulfillment of the objective. Small groups make the church mobile and resilient. A church that has loyal and unified small groups can accomplish just about anything!

> **A CHURCH THAT HAS LOYAL AND UNIFIED SMALL GROUPS CAN ACCOMPLISH JUST ABOUT ANYTHING!**

WARNING: It is really easy for a small group to forget that they are part of a bigger church vision and try to become independent. This kind of mindset is the beginning of division. The small group was never created to cause division, but to fulfill the vision. The small group leader must make it a habit on a weekly basis to refer and remind the group of the church's vision and constantly ask themselves how they can play a part in making sure that the vision comes to pass.

GOAL #8 - MULTIPLICATION - EXPONENTIAL GROWTH HAPPENS IN SMALL GROUPS

If we follow Jesus' pattern of discipleship, we will be setting up our churches to be able to grow exponentially. Jesus' pattern of discipleship was simple. The first step was recruiting 12 disciples. Jesus was intentional about making disciples. If you asked Him, who was He discipling He would have given you 12 names.

IF WE FOLLOW JESUS' PATTERN OF DISCIPLESHIP, WE WILL BE SETTING UP OUR CHURCHES TO BE ABLE TO GROW EXPONENTIALLY.

Matthew 10:2-3 (NKJV)
Now the names of the twelve apostles are these: first, Simon, who is called Peter, and Andrew his brother; James the son of Zebedee, and John his brother; 3 Philip and Bartholomew; Thomas and Matthew the tax collector; James the son of Alphaeus, and Lebbaeus, whose surname was Thaddaeus;

If that same question was asked to the average believer today, they would not be able to answer with specific names. I think we have forgotten Jesus' original mission for the church was to make disciples of all nations. Jesus was not giving us a suggestion but He was showing us our purpose and giving us a system to reach the whole world. The scope of the mission was all nations. This was no small task but He gave us everything we needed to accomplish it. He gave us His Word, the Holy Spirit and instructions on how to fulfill it. Let's look at the original instructions.

Matthew 28:18-20 (NLT)
Jesus came and told his disciples, "I have been given all authority in heaven and on earth. 19 Therefore, go

and make disciples of all the nations, baptizing them in the name of the Father and the Son and the Holy Spirit. 20 Teach these new disciples to obey all the commands I have given you. And be sure of this: I am with you always, even to the end of the age."

When Jesus recruited His twelve disciples, He recruited them with a vision of reaching others. He didn't say follow me and you will be the happiest person on earth or follow me and you will never have any problems again, but He said, "Follow me and I will make you fishers of men."

Matthew 4:19 (NLT)
Jesus called out to them, "Come, follow me, and I will show you how to fish for people!"

Jesus showed His disciples how to reach and disciple the whole world. The plan that Jesus left us to disciple others was simple and duplicatable; recruit, care, train and send. As long as the disciples followed this pattern they would be able to carry out the great commission. A true disciple of Jesus Christ is expected to teach and live like Him. The goal isn't just to know what Jesus taught but also to be like our teacher and teach others to do so.

A TRUE DISCIPLE OF JESUS CHRIST IS EXPECTED TO TEACH AND LIVE LIKE HIM.

Luke 6:40 (NLT)
Students are not greater than their teacher. But the student who is fully trained will become like the teacher.

Just imagine if we did it just like Jesus, the growth would be massive. There is exponential power to grow in Jesus model of discipleship. Below is a diagram of the potential growth we can experience if we follow Jesus' pattern of discipleship through small groups of 12. These examples are meant to open up our minds to what is possible if we carried out the example Jesus left us at the highest level of application.

1ST LEVEL - WE RECRUIT TWELVE DISCIPLES JUST LIKE JESUS DID

Imagine if we only had one assignment in our lifetime and that was to recruit and disciple just 12 people. Would that assignment be unfair or impossible? I believe if we asked the average Christian today, "Do you believe that you could build relationships and recruit 12 disciples if you were given a lifetime to do it?" Most people would say, "Of course... and I think I could do more than that." Then why are we not doing it? We are not recruiting and discipling others because we have lost our focus on our purpose.

The next question that is pertinent to discipling others is, "Do you believe that you could train your 12 to recruit and train 12 if you had a lifetime to do it?" I believe we would get another affirmative answer. This second question is where most small groups fall short. They may get to 12 people attending, but they never expect their disciples to eventually make disciples themselves. It is so easy for our small group to turn into a place where we make friends but not a place where we empower people to be disciple makers themselves. Our goal should be to make disciples of Jesus Christ that make disciples of Jesus Christ. Read the previous sentence again and let it sink in.

OUR GOAL SHOULD BE TO MAKE DISCIPLES OF JESUS CHRIST THAT MAKE DISCIPLES OF JESUS CHRIST.

> "Our goal should be to make disciples of Jesus Christ that make disciples of Jesus Christ."

There are two parts to this powerful sentence; the first part is to make disciples. The second part brings it around full circle. This is where our disciples make disciples. We don't just train people to know, but we train people to do. Now, let's look at the basic math and potential multiplication if we just make disciples of Jesus Christ that make disciples of Jesus Christ.

MATH: 1 + 12 = 13

NOTE: One person recruits 12. At the first level, we have one small group of 12 and the leader which makes it 13. I believe anyone can do this. What do you think?

2ND LEVEL - TRAIN THE 12 TO RECRUIT 12 DISCIPLES OF THEIR OWN

At this level the original 12 turn into 144+13=157 Just imagine the potential growth we would experience if we taught the church to recruit disciples the way Jesus did and taught them to teach others to do the same.

MATH: 12×12=144 +13=157 (The original twelve have been trained to recruit 12.)

3RD LEVEL - THE ORIGINAL 12 TRAIN THEIR 12 TO RECRUIT 12

At this level the original 12 is now over 1800 disciples. Wow!!! Let's look at the basic math.

MATH: 144 × 12 = 1728 +157 = 1885 disciples

NOTE: The 157 are the leaders from first two levels.

Jesus has given us a plan through small groups of 12 to impact the whole world. There is exponential power in discipling 12 people to disciple 12 people. Do these numbers blow your mind? At the 3rd level we now have the potential to take care and disciple over 1800 people. I am not saying this is going to be easy, but it is possible!

Mark 9:23(NKJV)
Jesus said to him, "If you can believe,
all things are possible to him who believes."

4TH LEVEL - THE 3RD LEVEL NOW DUPLICATES THEMSELVES.

This is where we start reaching thousands of people. This type of movement can capture a whole city and even start a worldwide revival. You might be saying, "Aren't you taking this a little too far? It looks like you want to reach the whole world!" Exactly! That is the point, Jesus gave us a commission to go into all the world. We need to get our thinking higher. Secular companies think "world dominance," why shouldn't we have the same aspirations?

THIS TYPE OF MOVEMENT CAN CAPTURE A WHOLE CITY AND EVEN START A WORLDWIDE REVIVAL.

Example, Facebook has 2.4 billion active users every month. Facebook isn't looking to just reach a few thousand people; they are aiming to reach the entire world. Why should secular companies have a global vision while the church remains thinking small and content with menial results? The math at the fourth level is mind blowing.

MATH: 1728 × 12 = 20,736 + 1885 = 22,621

At four levels of leadership development we are now discipling 22,621 people for Jesus. These numbers would place your church among the largest churches in America. A church that disciples like Jesus is guaranteed to grow. In this system of developing disciples and leaders, no one person is directly responsible for more than 12 people. The truth is none of us can personally disciple 22,621 people but we can do it through others that are willing to disciple 12. There is no limit of what Jesus can do through a trained church that has accepted its call to make disciples of all nations.

> **A CHURCH THAT DISCIPLES LIKE JESUS IS GUARANTEED TO GROW.**

In order to multiply, we must train every member of the small group to be a leader themselves and recruit 12 of their own. We should never teach just for the sake of teaching, but teach with the goal of empowering the people to disciple others themselves. The modern day church has done an awful job of equipping the church body for the work of the ministry. We need to make it our mission to make disciples that in turn make disciples. A small group can turn into a pond instead of a mighty river giving life to others throughout the world. A small group remains a pond when the commission to make disciples is not passed on to each member of the group. Every member of a small group should know that they are expected to eventually recruit 12 disciples of their own and train them to make disciples. Without the weight of discipleship passed onto the members of the group, we are creating weak, small minded disciples that feel that they have no purpose of their own. Multiplication happens when each member of our team goes out and creates a small group of 12 of their own disciples. Multiplication happens when a healthy small group, turns into two small groups. In a perfect world, the multiplication process continues and eventually every member of our small group leads a small group themselves. Multiplication is always the goal. We should never start a small group without the intention of training everyone in the group to be a disciple maker and small group leader. You might be asking, "How do I begin the process of establishing small groups and multiplication as part of our church growth systems?" Let's discover the answer in our next chapter!

CHAPTER SEVENTEEN
HOW TO BUILD PRINCIPLE #8
"SEVEN STEPS TO START A SMALL GROUP MINISTRY IN YOUR CHURCH"

CHAPTER 17

HOW TO BUILD PRINCIPLE # 8

SEVEN STEPS TO START A SMALL GROUP MINISTRY IN YOUR CHURCH

STEP 1 - THE LEAD PASTOR MUST BE ON BOARD.

Until the pastor is on board, small groups won't work. The pastor must be the one who is carrying and proclaiming the vision. Whatever the pastor is excited about is what the church will eventually be excited about. The pastor needs to be the first one to recruit 12 disciples and build a team that makes its main focus to build small groups.

STEP 2 - CREATE A SMALL GROUP LEADERSHIP TEAM THAT DISCUSSES AND DEFINES WHAT SMALL GROUPS ARE GOING TO LOOK LIKE IN THE CHURCH.

With every dream, we must build a team. At the beginning of the process this leadership team is gathering information, defining what small group ministry should look like and putting everything in writing. Every member of this leadership team must be willing to lead a small group themselves. This leadership team is responsible for creating the training manual, launching strategy, and the success of small group initiatives.

STEP 3 - CHOOSE A SMALL GROUP COORDINATOR OR PASTOR THAT LEADS THE SMALL GROUP MINISTRY OF CHURCH.

This leader should be chosen from the original small group leadership team. He must also have a great desire to build the local church through small groups and have a proven track record of being a team builder and people person. This leader will be responsible for recruiting, training, and achieving all small group initiatives and goals.

STEP 4 - SHARE VISION WITH ALL LEADERS IN CHURCH.

The best way to share the vision is to have a big leadership meeting with every leader in the church present. The vision should only be shared after the pastor of the church and small group leadership team is one-hundred percent sold on moving forward. Another key component that must be in place before presenting it to all the leaders is a strategic plan on how small groups will be implemented into the fiber of the church.

STEP 5 - START SMALL GROUP LEADERSHIP TRAINING WITH PRESENT LEADERS.

Every ministry and team leader must understand the new culture. Everyone in a position of leadership will also be required to be a small group leader and disciple maker. This means that leaders will not only be responsible for day to day ministry activities, but they will also be responsible for lovingly caring for and discipling each member of the team by developing small groups within the ministry. During this training time, each leader needs to determine what type of small group they are going to lead. Will it be a ministry focused small group, a special interest small group, a couples small group, a discipleship small group, a women's or men's small group, etc? This will help those that are interested in joining a small group determine which group best fits them.

STEP 6 - SET A LAUNCH DATE AND PRESENT ALL NEW LEADERS TO THE CONGREGATION.

The leaders should be present and be available after service to connect and recruit people to teams. Remember, most people need to be asked to join a group. Everyone wants to feel wanted. We must train our leaders to make people feel important and needed.

> **EVERYONE WANTS TO FEEL WANTED. WE MUST TRAIN OUR LEADERS TO MAKE PEOPLE FEEL IMPORTANT AND NEEDED.**

STEP 7 - MAKE SMALL GROUPS PART OF THE GROWTH TRACK FOR CHURCH.

Small groups should not be treated as an option, but as a necessary step to spiritual development. As a church, we introduce small groups at every level of our growth track. We should also have a connection zone, a place where the church can ask questions and join a small group. This connection zone should be manned and open before and after every service. Our websites and church apps should also have easy ways for our people to connect to small groups. God has some wonderful plans for growth that we can only discover in a small group setting. Let's get ready to grow!

BONUS SECTION

THREE STEPS TO HELP PEOPLE OPEN UP IN SMALL GROUPS

STEP 1 - START THE CONVERSATION BY FINDING SOME COMMON GROUND.

John 4:7 (NLT)
"Soon a Samaritan woman came to draw water, and Jesus said to her, 'Please give me a drink.' 8 He was alone at the time because his disciples had gone into the village to buy some food."

Jesus found common ground immediately with the woman at the well. The common ground was the water in the well. We can't expect those that are new to the group to just open up. It's our responsibility as leaders to start the conversation. People don't open up until trust is built and this trust will only be built through conversations. The goal of every small group leader must be to develop a personal relationship with each individual on the team. The first time someone opens up might not be during the small group bible study time, they might be more willing to open up in a one-on-one conversation with the leader or a member of small group. A small group will never be effective if it doesn't turn into a dialogue. A small group meeting should never be run like a regular church service where the pastor is teaching and everyone else is just listening. Jesus knew that in order for this Samaritan woman to receive from Him, He first needed to get her to speak to Him. Let's not wait for them to engage with us. We as leaders and believers should be the ones initiating the conversations.

STEP 2 - MAKE SURE THAT THEY FEEL NEEDED AND IMPORTANT.

Jesus does this by asking her for some help. This woman couldn't believe that he was speaking to her because of two main reasons: First, she was a woman. Second, she was a Samaritan. Jesus lets this woman know that she is important by engaging her in a conversation and that she is needed by asking her for some water. She was also surprised that He spoke to her because at this time in her life she hardly had anyone to speak to because of her colored past. She had a reputation of going from man to man, which would have made her an outcast in her society and that's probably why she was there all alone in the middle of the day drawing water. Despite all of the mistakes that she made and the negative thoughts everyone had about her, Jesus reaches out to her and makes her feel important and needed.

There are many people around us that are guilt ridden and outcasts in our society that need someone to engage with them in conversation and invite them to be part of something bigger than themselves.

> **THERE ARE MANY PEOPLE AROUND US THAT ARE GUILT RIDDEN AND OUTCASTS IN OUR SOCIETY THAT NEED SOMEONE TO ENGAGE WITH THEM IN CONVERSATION AND INVITE THEM TO BE PART OF SOMETHING BIGGER THAN THEMSELVES.**

John 4:9 (NLT)
"The woman was surprised, for Jews refuse to have anything to do with Samaritans. She said to Jesus, 'You are a Jew, and I am a Samaritan woman. Why are you asking me for a drink?' 10 Jesus replied, 'If you only knew the gift God has for you and who you are speaking to, you would ask me, and I would give you living water.'"

STEP 3 - ALLOW THEM TO TALK AND ASK QUESTIONS.

This was not a one-way conversation. This was a clear dialogue. Jesus says something, then she says something. Notice that Jesus doesn't cut her off in mid-sentence. He acknowledges what she says and responds accordingly. At the end of the conversation, a miracle happens, she ends up coming to the conclusion that Jesus is the Messiah, the promised Savior. She is so convinced that she ends up going to the village and shares her encounter with everyone, and the whole village becomes believers. I hope that we can see the correlation. When someone opens up in a small group, they will also begin to open up publicly about Jesus. When that happens, the church begins to rapidly multiply.

WHEN SOMEONE OPENS UP IN A SMALL GROUP, THEY WILL ALSO BEGIN TO OPEN UP PUBLICLY ABOUT JESUS.

John 4:11-26 (NLT)
"'But sir, you don't have a rope or a bucket,' she said, 'and this well is very deep. Where would you get this living water? 12 And besides, do you think you're greater than our ancestor Jacob, who gave us this well? How can you offer better water than he and his sons and his animals enjoyed?' 13 Jesus replied, 'Anyone who drinks this water will soon become thirsty again. 14 But those who drink the water I give will never be thirsty again. It becomes a fresh, bubbling spring within them, giving them eternal life.' 15 'Please, sir,' the woman said, 'give me this water! Then I'll never be thirsty again, and I won't have to come here to get water.' 16 'Go and

get your husband,' Jesus told her. 17 'I don't have a husband,' the woman replied. Jesus said, 'You're right! You don't have a husband— 18 for you have had five husbands, and you aren't even married to the man you're living with now. You certainly spoke the truth!' 19 'Sir,' the woman said, 'you must be a prophet. 20 So tell me, why is it that you Jews insist that Jerusalem is the only place of worship, while we Samaritans claim it is here at Mount Gerizim, where our ancestors worshiped?' 21 Jesus replied, 'Believe me, dear woman, the time is coming when it will no longer matter whether you worship the Father on this mountain or in Jerusalem. 22 You Samaritans know very little about the one you worship, while we Jews know all about him, for salvation comes through the Jews. 23 But the time is coming—indeed it's here now—when true worshipers will worship the Father in spirit and in truth. The Father is looking for those who will worship him that way. 24 For God is Spirit, so those who worship him must worship in spirit and in truth.' 25 The woman said, 'I know the Messiah is coming—the one who is called Christ. When he comes, he will explain everything to us.' 26 Then Jesus told her, 'I am the Messiah!'"

John 4:39 (NLT) "Many Samaritans from the village believed in Jesus because the woman had said, 'He told me everything I ever did!'"

Jesus masterfully causes this woman that was considered an outcast to open up. I can't overemphasize the value of people opening up in our small groups. This interaction with Jesus gave her the confidence to boldly share her faith with everyone in her village. The end result of just one small group meeting with Jesus is a whole village that ended up believing in Jesus as their Lord and Savior. In this story, we see the power and potential of a small group and how it can lead to massive kingdom growth. Small groups are such a great place for our people to develop the confidence that they need to share their faith. As they become comfortable with opening up and sharing in the safe environment of friends, they will gain the boldness to talk about what Jesus has done for them with others.

> **SMALL GROUPS ARE SUCH A GREAT PLACE FOR OUR PEOPLE TO DEVELOP THE CONFIDENCE THAT THEY NEED TO SHARE THEIR FAITH.**

CHAPTER 17

ACTION PLAN

FOR CARING FOR PEOPLE THROUGH VIBRANT SMALL GROUPS

LIST 5 THINGS YOU CAN APPLY FROM THIS CHAPTER TO EXPERIENCE GUARANTEED GROWTH

#1

#2

#3

#4

#5

CONCLUSION

I pray that these 8 Principles for "Guaranteed Growth" will help you build a ministry or organization that is healthy, well balanced and continually growing. I love you and will be praying for you and your ministry every day. Get ready to see Guaranteed Growth!

GUARANTEEDGROWTH.LIFE

- Visit Our Website For Information

- Request And Download Templates
  Resources@GuaranteedGrowth.Life

- Read Articles And Testimonials

- Access The Latest Teaching And Topic From Pastor Marco

EMAIL US YOUR STORY

- Please Give Us The Privilege Of Hearing How The Guaranteed Growth Book Has Impacted You And Your Organization.
Story@GuaranteedGrowth.Life

CPSIA information can be obtained
at www.ICGtesting.com
Printed in the USA
BVHW041750260622
640683BV00009B/29